KU-501-622

CONTENTS

The Long Term *Effects* of Being a Carer

WITHDRAWN

by
Ruth Hancock
Claire Jarvis

LIBRARY
LOTHIAN COLLEGE OF HEALTH STUDIES
13 CREWE ROAD SOUTH
EDINBURGH
EH4 2LD

Age Concern Institute of Gerontology, King's College London

Lon

NAPIER UNIVERSITY

COM 649.8 HAN

© Crown copyright 1994

Applications for reproduction should be made to HMSO

First published 1994

0 11 321886 9

THE AGE CONCERN INSTITUTE OF GERONTOLOGY, *Kings College London*

The Age Concern Institute of Gerontology at King's College London was established in 1986 as a joint venture with Age Concern England, to engage in teaching and research into ageing and issues which affect elderly people. Director: Professor Anthea Tinker.

ABOUT THE AUTHORS

The authors are both researchers at the Age Concern Institute of Gerontology, King's College London.

Ruth Hancock is an economist, with a particular interest in social security, pensions and financial well-being in later life. Claire Jarvis is a data analyst, with a special interest in research using household surveys and population statistics.

They also run the *Gerontology Data Service*, which provides data and analysis relating to older people.

List of Tables

List of Figures

ACKNOWLEDGEMENTS

The research on which this book is based was conducted over a six month period starting in December 1993 and ending at the end of May 1994. We would like to thank the Baring Foundation for a grant which enabled it to take place. Material from the *Survey of Retirement and Retirement Plans*, made available through the Office of Population Censuses and Surveys, has been used by permission of the controller general of HMSO. Analysis of the survey was conducted through the Gerontology Data Service at ACIOG, King's College London. The grant holders were Professor Anthea Tinker and Dr Janet Askham and the research has been conducted by Ruth Hancock and Dr Claire Jarvis.

We wish to express our gratitude to Anthea Tinker and Janet Askham for guidance and comments on previous drafts of this book. All responsibility for the analysis and interpretation of data reported here – and any errors – rests with us alone.

Ruth Hancock and Claire Jarvis.

INTRODUCTION

As people enter middle or older age their lives are often described in terms of loss of jobs or relationships; they lose jobs, parental responsibilities, spouses through death, children through geographical migration. These losses are often studied as potential problem areas: how do people cope after marriage has ended or after they have retired? It is surprising therefore that the cessation of caring for a sick, disabled or elderly relative has rarely been studied in the same way. For caregiving – as is well-known – is also in our society an increasingly common social role. And, although an enormous amount is now known about caring itself, very little is known about being an ex-carer. Yet it is a fascinating and important subject. Since caregiving can occupy time, emotions, physical and economic resources (just as jobs and marriage can), any cessation is bound to have implications. Of course these may be very positive; research shows how stressful caring can be: shedding a burden is a relief or even a positive delight. It may release the spare bedroom; it may save on heating bills; one's health may improve; there will be more time and energy to spare for other activities – for new relationships, a full-time job, a move to a new area. But the opposite may also be true; just as even the ending of a stressful marriage relationship or a demanding job can bring problems of adjustment, so can the end of caring. For caring will have left its mark, a mark which may endure. The loss of the caring identity may be the most difficult to cope with emotionally, but almost equally important is the possibility of lasting effects on: health, job and career advancement opportunities, one's chances of marrying, the number of children one will have, one's financial position in retirement, and so on.

Of course these effects will vary enormously because carers are so diverse: a relatively young single person who had cared for a parent will be affected differently, by ceasing to care, from a married woman who had looked after her disabled adult child or frail parent, or the elderly husband who had cared for his wife. And, of course, some of the things which will happen to them after caring will not be direct consequences of caregiving itself, but will be part of the more general pattern of their lives, patterns which may indeed help to explain why they became carers in the first place. For example a person with limited prospects of paid employment may be more likely to become a carer than one with good prospects; ceasing to care could throw him or her back into the same unfriendly job market. The same might perhaps be said about the marriage market for some.

So, a long-term or life-course perspective is ideally needed to study life after caring.

This book reports the results of research whose aims have been to examine the circumstances of people who have at some time in the past acted as informal carers of a sick, handicapped or elderly relative or friend. While considerable research has been undertaken on the contemporary consequences of caring, little is known, on a national scale, about what happens to carers once their caring responsibilities have ceased. In 1988 the Office of Population Censuses and Surveys, on behalf of the Department of Social Security, undertook a nationally representative survey of people aged 55–69 which provides a rare opportunity to investigate how people had combined caring with employment, marriage and child-bearing over the course of their lives. This data source forms the basis of the research reported here which in turn builds on previous analysis of the data, conducted within the Age Concern Institute of Gerontology (ACIOG) (Askham *et al.*, 1992).

The research has been centred around a number of questions, specifically:
- What has been the effect of caring on the incomes of past carers?
- What has been the effect of caring on employment and pension histories?
- What is the subsequent pattern of marriage and, for women, of child bearing?
- How many past carers move home after caring ceases and for what reasons?

In each case, we have sought to investigate the role of factors such as gender, age, marital and employment status and the nature of caring, so far as data permit.

We are fortunate in having some information on carers' own views on the effects caring has had on their lives. However, we must stress that in other respects we cannot be sure that an apparent 'effect' of caring is indeed that, rather than a reflection of the kinds of people who take on caring responsibilities in the first place.

The report is organised in the following way. Chapter One sets out the background and findings from previous research on current carers. Chapter Two describes the data source on which our research draws, presents basic sample characteristics and an analysis of the self-reported effects of caring. In Chapter Three we describe the results of detailed analysis of the current incomes of past carers. An exploration of the relationship between caring, employment and pension histories is contained in Chapter Four. In Chapter Five we analyse patterns of marriage, child-bearing and house moves of past carers. The final chapter – Chapter Six – concludes with a summary of our findings and a discussion of some of the issues which arise and conclusions which may be drawn. Further details on data and methodology can be found in the appendix.

1 BACKGROUND AND PREVIOUS RESEARCH

INFORMAL CARE: PRESENT AND FUTURE

Informal care, especially of elderly people, is an issue of major importance for people interested in social policy today. At present there are estimated to be around 6.8 million adults in Britain caring for sick, handicapped or elderly people, and around one in five of these carers spends at least 20 hours a week providing care and assistance (OPCS, 1992). Analysis of large-scale survey data has identified three groups of people heavily involved in the care of elderly people - married women under retirement age, single adult children, and elderly spouse carers. Although a substantial proportion of the total volume of informal care (around a third) is provided by the latter, a quarter is provided by people who are under the age of 45 (Arber and Ginn, 1991).

Demographic trends ensure that informal care will remain at the forefront of the attention of policy makers and researchers in social policy. Although relatively constant in the near future, the numbers and proportions of elderly people are projected to rise significantly in the longer term.

Table 1: Numbers and proportions of the population aged 65 and over; England, 1991–2021

Year	Population (000s)				% total population aged:			
	65–74	75–84	85+	65+	65–74	75–84	85+	65+
1991	4,231	2,622	765	7,618	8.8	5.5	1.6	15.9
2001	4,039	2,736	1,022	7,797	8.1	5.5	2.0	15.6
2011	4,511	2,748	1,220	8,479	8.8	5.4	2.4	16.6
2021	5,369	3,275	1,366	10,010	10.3	6.3	2.6	19.2

Source: OPCS, 1991-based population projections, national projections, series PP2, 18, September 1993 (microfiche)

Although, in the next ten years, the number of people aged 65 to 74 in England will actually decline, a further 371,000 will be added to the population aged over 75. Whilst only one person in 14 is over 75 today, in thirty years' time, an estimated one person in 11 will be over 75. This is a matter of considerable importance, as physical and mental disability and the need for care rises rapidly with age. Today, 41% of people aged 75 and over in Britain are moderately or severely disabled (Evandrou, 1987). Assuming the same age-specific disability levels over time, a simple calculation on the figures in Table 1 suggests that in England in thirty years' time there will be more than half a million extra moderately or severely disabled people over the age of 75, and who will probably be in need of care of some sort. Although it is unlikely that elderly spouse carers will become less willing or able to care for their sick or disabled partners, the ability of the other main caring groups (married women and adult children), who are at present most likely to provide informal care for sick and elderly people, may well diminish. Although there is evidence that this is not happening yet, the combination of smaller family size and greater geographical mobility may reduce the number of adult children living near their parents, whilst changing employment patterns – a reduction in full-time male employment, and an increase in part-time female employment – means that women have become increasingly recognised as joint breadwinners, and may find it more difficult to combine paid work with high levels of care-giving. A less gloomy picture, however, is painted by Grundy (1992), at least for the supply of care for elderly people.

Government policy is geared towards care in the community, and explicitly relies on a pool of people prepared to provide unpaid care and support; it assumes that this pool of carers will always be available to care. As the role of statutory services in caring for frail elderly people is very limited, and is generally targeted at people who live alone (Evandrou *et al.*, 1986), the capacity of the community to cope with any increases in the need for informal care needs to be determined. Problems that might be caused by the changing demographic situation must be faced with some urgency (see, for example, FPSC, 1989; Laczko and Noden, 1991), and different care alternatives assessed.

A recent report commissioned by the Department of Health notes that

> "... for many carers, support is provided only at a cost to themselves,
> i.e. cost of lost employment opportunities, lost financial security, or
> physical and mental ill-health ..." (Department of Health, 1991:8)

Such emotional and financial burdens have an immediate impact on carers, but the issues of today are as much the issues of the future as demographic trends. The effect of caring on employment, by forcing employees to forgo training and promotion opportunities, reduce working hours, or even give up paid work (Parker, 1990) is particularly important, as the way in which caring affects employment today will have an effect on the future pensions, and hence the future living standards and the necessity for state benefits of carers for decades to come.

Government policy does to some extent recognise the need to protect current incomes and future retirement pensions of informal carers, but the social security provision for informal carers has been described as 'still not comprehensive in coverage, coherent in design, or adequate in level' (Glendinning, 1988:136), and it has been argued that the economic consequences of informal caring, at the level of the individual, remain largely unacknowledged in the development of community care policies (Glendinning, 1992:3). Employees have no statutory right to special leave, and may have to use holiday entitlements, their own sick leave, or the goodwill of their employer to cope with emergencies arising from their caring responsibilities. Despite some recent extension of benefits for carers, there is no benefit entitlement for carers who engage in more than a modest level of paid employment (the entitlement to Invalid Care Allowance is lost if the claimant does work which earns him/her more than £50 a week), and as entitlement to all 'carer benefits' (Invalid Care Allowance, crediting of National Insurance contributions, and Home Responsibilities Protection of retirement pension rights) depends on the receipt of the Attendance Allowance by the dependant person, most carers receive no benefits at all. In 1988, only 110,000 carers received the ICA (HM Treasury, 1989), around 11% of all eligible informal carers, i.e. those providing more than 35 hours a week care (Baldwin, 1994). In 1992 the figure stood at 189,000 (DSS, 1993) but this is still small in relation to the number of carers. A priority, according to many researchers, is to make government and employers more aware of the effects of care-giving on employment (see, for example, Laczko and Phillipson, 1991). This is difficult in the absence of useful data.

THE IMPACT OF CARING ON PRESENT LIVES

In 1985 more than one in ten full-time workers were carers of elderly, sick or handicapped people, as were nearly two fifths of part-time workers (Green, 1988). The socio-economic position of current carers has received recent attention (see, for example, Parker, 1989; Glendinning, 1989; Arber and Ginn, 1990; and Joshi, 1994), and most research has concluded that caring has an impact on employment and income, though the apparent effect is often small. Parker and Lawton's analysis of the 1985 General Household Survey (GHS) identified two main effects of caring on carers' personal earnings. Firstly, there is an overall depressive effect because carers are less likely to be in paid work; secondly, carers actually in work have lower earnings because of their shorter hours (Parker and Lawton, 1990), and possibly lower hourly rates of pay (Joshi, 1994). Parker and Lawton (1990) concluded that carers in general were less likely to be employed than their matched sample of non-carers (a reduction in the employment rate of 3 percentage points for women, and 7 percentage points for men). In a similar analysis, Evandrou and Winter (1992) found a reduction in the employment rate of 3% for women and 5% for men. Evandrou (1991) found only a small difference in the income distribution of carers and non-carers, with 19% of carers in the bottom quintile income group, compared with 18% of non-carers.

Looking at carers as a single group, however, obscures the very real differences *between* carers, and the apparent impact of caring on their lives (see Twigg and Atkin, 1994, for a review of the research on the origin, incidence, pattern and experience of caring). Although one must be wary of attributing causality, particularly when using cross-sectional data, four factors have been identified which seem to account for most of the apparent differences in the impact of caring on the financial circumstances of carers.

Gender. Until recently, caring was viewed very much as a female activity. This claim has been challenged by analysis of the GHS 1985 carers' data, and by some small-scale research which suggests that men care for kin in similar ways to women (Parker, 1989). However, the nature and level of caring responsibilities and their effects do seem to be different for male and female carers. Caring is very rarely taken on by men at the expense of employment, whereas most women, at some time in their life, take on caring responsibilities which limit their earning capacity (Joshi, 1987). An analysis of the Labour Force Survey showed that in 1986 one in six women who had left employment in the previous three years had done so in order to care for a family member (Laczko and Phillipson, 1991). The number of men doing so was very small. (An initial analysis of the Retirement Survey, however, has shown that quite a large proportion, one in ten, of co-resident current male carers had ever left a job to care for a sick, disabled or elderly relative; this compares with 18% of women; Askham *et al.*, 1992, Table 3.6.) Women are more likely to be sole carers, caring for 20 or more hours a week, and caring over extended periods (Evandrou, 1991). Equal Opportunities Commission research shows that women carry heavier burdens of care, and that male carers receive more informal and service support (Charlesworth *et al.*, 1984). The majority of male carers are caring for spouses, and intergenerational care, which involves long hours and intimate personal care is still overwhelmingly carried out by women (Twigg and Atkin, 1994). Joshi (1994) suggests that caring for an elderly relative has a similar effect on the labour market participation of women as the care of children. The employment consequences of this are well known: fewer women are in employment than men, and more work on a part-time basis (22% of women under 60 worked part-time in 1991, compared with under 1% of men; Joshi, 1994). The by-products of part-time work – poor rates of pay, job insecurity, and insufficient pension coverage – therefore affect women to a far greater extent than men.

Residence. In 1990, two-thirds of carers who had a dependant living in their own household were spending at least 20 hours a week caring, compared with only 10% of those whose dependants did not live in (OPCS, 1992). An analysis of GHS 1985 found that people caring for dependants within the household earned lower mean hourly wages compared with the average for all non-carers, both for men and women (Evandrou and Winter, 1986). Twenty-five per cent of carers with dependants in the same household were in the bottom income quintile, compared with 16% of carers caring for someone outside the household. Joshi (1994) concluded that being the sole carer of a co-resident dependant reduced female and male employment rates by 67 and 29 percentage points respectively.

Type of care provided. The nature of caring tasks which may be provided varies a great deal. People may provide help anywhere along the caring spectrum from help with filling in forms through to continuous, intimate personal care; all may be described as providing informal care and support. It is also important to know whether or not the caring is a shared responsibility (whether caring is a sole, joint or peripheral responsibility). Sole carers are more likely to be in the bottom income quintile groups (21%, compared with 11% of joint carers; Evandrou, 1991:18).

Amount of time spent caring. Both the frequency of care, and the length of time spent caring, have an impact on the employment and income of carers. Caring which lasts a few months will probably not be a great financial burden, whereas caring which lasts several years almost undoubtedly will (Askham *et al*, 1992). Most carers (58%) spend less than 10 hours a week caring for someone, but 11% spend more than 50 hours a week caring (OPCS, 1992). Caring for more than 50 hours a week apparently had the effect of reducing female and male labour force participation rates by 16% and 14% respectively (Joshi, 1994).

Carers are clearly a varied group; this explains why cross-tabulations comparing all carers with non-carers often reveal only small differences in employment rates and income. As the large majority of carers are not co-resident, and provide less than 12 hours a week care, this is not surprising. However, the effects of caring do apparently have a considerable impact on the small hard-core of co-resident carers who provide more than 50 hours care per week. It is this hard core which may grow in number as more elderly people need to be cared for, for longer, in the community (Joshi, 1994:7).

PROBLEMS WITH CURRENT RESEARCH

Many of the studies which attempt to examine the effects of caring on the lives of carers are very small (see, for example, Glendinning, 1988; Nissel and Bonnerjea, 1982), are not intended to be nationally representative, and lack control groups of non-carers; most of these studies have focused on women and people who are not in employment (Laczko and Noden, 1992). It is qualitative work of this kind which often reports the severest financial disadvantages and restrictions on employment (see Parker, 1990, for a review). Retrospective analysis of carers' work histories, for example, show that combining care and work can be very difficult; all of the daughters who continued to work in Lewis and Meredith's study (1988) reported a conflict between caring and work. Glendinning (1992), in semi-structured interviews with 30 carers found that caring did have an effect on employment, but the effects were very varied. Because of the nature of the sample selection in this sort of research, however, it is not possible to extrapolate results from these surveys to the population as a whole.

Large-scale surveys overcome the problem of small sample sizes and national representativeness, but mean that analysis is restricted to the small number of questions asked of carers in government-sponsored surveys. It is not possible to test the claims made in qualitative research about the financial consequences of care-giving on these data for the general population. A serious problem, when one is limited to cross-sectional data, is the difficulty of analysing the direction of causality. It is also impossible to assess the impact of present caring on future lives, despite the important issues involved for individuals and governments. There are no large-scale longitudinal surveys of carers. Little is known, therefore, either about the immediate effect of ceasing to care (for example, the financial costs associated with the loss of benefits paid in respect of a dependant, and the necessity of looking for work with little recent job experience; McLaughlin, 1991); or about the long-term effects associated with low pensions and low standards of living of carers in later life. We know that the majority of carers under pensionable age remain in employment (Laczko and Noden, 1993), but we know little about the effect of combining caring and work on employment. While it may be true that

> "The economic position of carers today may have a direct impact on
> their financial position, as well as general quality of life, in their own
> old age" (Evandrou and Winter, 1989: 3),

we do not have the tools at our disposal to examine the thesis in any depth. The Retirement Survey is a large-scale, cross-sectional survey but, unlike the General Household Survey, it also contains information on past carers, and retrospective information on pension and work histories. A preliminary analysis of third age carers has suggested that former carers are financially disadvantaged in later life (Tinker *et al.*, 1992), and has underlined the need for further research on the effects of caring on the future lives of carers.

This study is an attempt to fill one of the important gaps in current research on the effects of caring on carers.

2 DATA AND BASIC SAMPLE CHARACTERISTICS

THE RETIREMENT SURVEY OF 1988

The source for our study is the *Survey of Retirement and Retirement Plans* (referred to here as the "Retirement Survey"), which was carried out by the Office of Population Censuses and Surveys in late 1988 and early 1989. The sample consists of around 3,500 people aged 55–69 and their partners outside that age group. It is a nationally representative survey of such people living in private households in Great Britain (see appendix for further information on sample sizes and weighting, and a comparison of the Retirement Survey with the 1991 census and the General Household Survey).

The purpose of the survey was to identify the factors affecting the age at retirement, gather information on the financial provisions that people make for retirement, and predict the distribution of future pensioners' incomes (Bone *et al.*, 1992). To this end, retrospective information on working lives and pensions was added to the more familiar cross-sectional data on current financial and other circumstances. Information was included on disability and caring, to test the possible effect of these factors on retirement income. Respondents were asked whether they were currently looking after, or providing some regular service for, a sick, elderly, or handicapped person. They were also asked whether they had 'ever in the past looked after someone (else) who was handicapped, elderly or suffering from long term illness?'

The sub-sample of past carers is respectably large (390 men and 713 women), but becomes uncomfortably small as we begin to classify our sample of past carers according to other factors of interest, such as retirement status and age. In some cases, therefore, differences between sub-groups are subject to considerable uncertainty and our analysis has to be restricted to broad classifications. Guidance on the levels of uncertainty is given through the use of formal statistical tests and the construction of confidence intervals. By convention such tests are conducted at the '90% (or greater) significance level' which may be regarded as somewhat stringent. For example, in certain areas, to be 70% sure that a difference exists between past carers and non-carers may be sufficient cause for concern. With a few exceptions, therefore, results are not suppressed even if they did not pass formal tests, although the reader's attention is drawn to the size of standard errors. With these provisos, the uniqueness of the Retirement Survey can be exploited to investigate the impact, in some detail, of past caring on future lives; an aspect of caring that has rarely been studied before.

In the remainder of this chapter, we use simple cross-tabulations to examine the stated effects of past caring on the lives of carers, and to look at some basic characteristics of carers. We then go on to explore in more detail the impact of past caring on future lives in subsequent chapters.

THE CHARACTERISTICS OF PAST CARERS

Women, and especially those who considered themselves retired[1], were over-represented amongst past carers. Men, particularly non-retired men, were under-represented. In all, nearly two-thirds of past carers were women, compared with 42% of non-carers; nearly a half (47%) were retired women, in contrast to 28% of non-carers. Only 13% of past carers were non-retired men; the corresponding figure for non-carers was 30%.

Table 2: Age composition of carers and non-carers; by gender and retirement status

Age	Men				Women			
	Retired		Non-retired		Retired		Non-retired	
	Past carer %	Non-carer %	Past carer %	Non-carer %	Past carer %	Non-carer %	Past carer %	Non-carer %
55–59	14	14	57	57	15	14	64	72
60–64	28	30	40	39	35	45	25	22
65–69	59	56	3	4	50	41	11	7
N	242	472	148	509	515	462	199	227

Source: Retirement Survey, Great Britain, 1988

Once retirement status is taken into account there was not a great deal of difference in the age distributions of past carers and non-carers, especially for men. For example, for retired male past carers, 14% were aged 55–59; the proportion was the same for retired male non-carers. For women, these were rather larger differences. Amongst retired female past carers, for example, one half were aged 65–69, compared with two-fifths of retired non-carers. Comparing non-retired women, 64% of past carers were in the age group 55–59 compared with 72% of non-carers. Marital status patterns also differed between past carers and non-carers.

Amongst men and women, retired and non-retired alike, past carers were less likely to be married, more likely to be widowed and, especially amongst men,

---

[1] The Retirement Survey used a self-assessed definition of retirement. For a full discussion see Bone *et al.* (1992).

Table 3: Marital status of carers and non-carers; by gender and retirement status

Age	Men				Women			
	Retired		Non-retired		Retired		Non-retired	
	Past carer %	Non-carer %	Past carer %	Non-carer %	Past carer %	Non-carer %	Past carer %	Non-carer %
Married	70	82	77	86	57	68	68	83
Single	13	5	13	5	9	5	6	3
Widowed	13	5	5	3	30	21	19	9
Divorced	5	8	5	6	5	5	7	5
N (base)	230	476	152	513	519	468	202	230

Source: Retirement Survey, Great Britain, 1988

more likely to be never-married. Over 80% of male non-carers were married, compared with 70% of retired past carers and 77% of non-retired past carers. Over two-thirds of retired female non-carers were married in contrast to 57% of past carers. Retired men who had been carers were almost three times as likely to be widowed as those who had not been carers. Amongst female past carers, a fifth of the non-retired and 30% of the retired were widows. The corresponding proportions amongst non-carers were 9% and 21% respectively.

A large proportion of both male and female past carers had spent a considerable length of time caring (Table 4). Only 5% of men and 6% of women had spent less than a year caring. One in ten had spent more than 20 years caring.

Table 4: Years spent caring; past carers, by gender

	proportions spending the following number of years caring:					
	<1 year	1–4	5–9	10–14	15–19	20+	N[2]
men	5	41	26	12	6	10	382
women	6	39	24	13	5	13	721

Source: Retirement Survey, Great Britain, 1988

---

[2] All sample numbers presented in tables are *unweighted* and may vary due to missing answers for some questions. Percentages, means, etc., are *weighted*. See appendix for further details.

Table 5: Whether caring had an effect on retirement plans; retired past carers, by gender and years spent caring

	proportion of those caring for the following number of years stating an effect on their retirement plans:				
	<5 years	5–9	10–19	20+	All
men (%)	7	10	4	4	7
N (base)	95	68	40	27	230
women (%)	5	13	17	15	10
N (base)	231	117	91	75	513
both (%)	5	12	13	12	9
N (base)	325	185	131	102	743

Source: Retirement Survey, Great Britain, 1988

Caring did not change the retirement plans of many past carers (Table 5). Overall, just under one in ten retired carers claimed that caring had had an effect on their retirement plans. The effect was stronger for women, with 16% of those who had cared for ten or more years claiming an effect. For men caring for ten years or more, the figure was much lower at 4%.

Differentials are more pronounced when looking at the numbers of all past carers who had ever given up a job and become unemployed because of their caring activities (Table 6). For men, no consistent effect according to the number of years spent caring is evident; 4% of men caring for less than five years had given up a job, whilst only 2% of men caring for more than 20 years had given up a job. It is true that overall a smaller proportion of men had given up a job and become unemployed, than claimed that caring affected their retirement plans, but for women the effect is much more marked, and is stronger according to the number of years spent caring. In all cases, the proportion of women affected was more than twice the proportion of men affected. Overall, more than one woman in seven claimed to have lost a job and become unemployed because of her caring responsibilities. Even for women caring for less than five years, one woman in eight was thus affected; for women caring for 20 or more years, one in four had lost a job because of caring responsibilities.

Lower proportions of both men and women had taken a lower paid job because of caring. In both cases, people caring for 20 or more years were most affected; but here the proportion was only 7%. Only 3% overall were affected. The proportions reporting difficulty getting a job were also small, with only 4% overall reporting difficulty. Even so, for women, one in ten of those caring for 20 or more years reported difficulty getting a job. More than double the numbers reported lost pay because of caring responsibilities, with

Table 6: Effects of caring on employment; past carers, by gender and years spent caring

	proportion of carers caring for the following number of years reporting stated effect on employment:				
	<5 years	5–9	10–19	20+	All
	carer lost job and became unemployed				
men (%)	4	6	3	2	4
N (base)	171	96	73	37	377
women (%)	13	13	18	24	15
N (base)	328	168	132	88	715
	carer took lower paid job				
men (%)	2	2	1	7	2
N (base)	169	96	72	37	374
women (%)	3	3	4	6	3
N (base)	323	166	129	87	705
	carer had difficulty getting a job				
men (%)	2	5	3	2	3
N (base)	169	96	73	37	375
women (%)	2	2	5	9	4
N (base)	323	166	129	87	705
	carer lost pay				
men (%)	9	9	13	10	10
N (base)	170	96	73	37	376
women (%)	7	10	14	20	11
N (base)	323	166	130	87	706
	carer reported at least one of the above effects				
men (%)	13	14	17	12	14
N (base)	169	96	72	37	374
women (%)	22	25	28	38	26
N (base)	323	166	130	87	705

Source: Retirement Survey, Great Britain, 1988

10% overall reporting a problem, and 20% of women who had cared for 20 or more years reporting lost pay.

The bottom section of Table 6 shows the proportions of people reporting at least one effect on employment (becoming unemployed, taking a lower paid job, having difficulty getting a job, or losing pay, or any combination of the four) because of their caring responsibilities. It is clear that although only modest proportions reported individual effects, overall quite substantial proportions found that caring had in some way affected their working lives. One man in seven found that caring had had some effect on his working life; there was not much difference across the 'years cared for' categories. Far more women reported an effect on their working lives. More than one in four overall claimed an effect, and there was considerable difference according to the number of years that caring responsibilities lasted. More than one in three of those caring for 20 or more years reported at least one effect.

We noted earlier that carers are a heterogeneous group, and that if they are examined as a single group of 'carers', the apparent effect of caring on other aspects of their lives will be small or non-existent. The above analysis of the basic characteristics of past carers is likely to demonstrate this. Only 14% of male carers reported any effect of caring on their working lives. It is unlikely that the other 86%, who did not report any difficulties, will exhibit marked differences from non-carers in their employment or income patterns. It therefore makes sense to examine carers who reported difficulties with work because of their caring responsibilities separately from those who reported no effects.

The self-stated effects of caring demonstrate the gender differentials which literature has reported. A large proportion of women carers (more than one in four of all past carers) reported a caring responsibility, quite apart from the usual caring responsibilities associated with childrearing, which in some way limited their earning capacity. A major drawback of the Retirement Survey, however, is that it is not possible to examine for past carers several of the other 'caring characteristics' which are believed to have an effect on employment (although there is more detailed information included for current carers; see Askham *et al.*, 1992, for a preliminary analysis). It has been found, for example, that the income levels of carers are strongly related to the place of residence of the dependant. The Retirement Survey contains no information on where the dependant was living. Likewise, there is no information on the nature of the caring tasks provided, on the number of hours a week spent caring, or on whether the carer was the sole carer, or shared responsibilities with others. The importance of this survey is that it is nationally representative, and the carer-characteristics that we do have are useful: gender, the number of years spent caring, some of the most important self-reported effects of caring, and the years in which caring began and ended. All of these can be tied in with general income level, and with detailed pension and work histories. We are in a position to begin to examine issues of considerable importance; in particular, to ask whether some carers are less well prepared for their own old age because of lower participation in paid employment during the period in which they were carers, and to investigate the longer term effects of being a carer.

LOTHIAN COLLEGE OF HEALTH STUDIES LIBRARY

3 CURRENT INCOMES OF PAST CARERS

The financial effects of caring are not necessarily confined to the period for which caring responsibilities last. The time immediately after caring ceases may be a time of hardship if the carer was financially dependent on the person for whom he or she was providing care. Since caring may also affect job and pay prospects, and the accumulation of pension rights and other benefits, the consequences can last longer still. In this section we contrast the incomes of past carers and non-carers to see what evidence exists concerning these longer-term financial effects of caring. We begin with a consideration of personal incomes, examining total income and its components – earnings, pensions, investment income and state benefits – and then go on to contrast the family incomes of non-carers and past carers.

PERSONAL INCOME

Incomes vary by gender and retirement status independently of the possible effects of caring. We therefore standardise for these factors throughout. However, the different patterns of marital status (and to a lesser extent age) found amongst past carers and non-carers also need to be borne in mind since these will also explain some of the differences in the incomes of past carers and non-carers.

General income level

Parker and Lawton (1990) found that caring appears to have an overall depressive effect on general income level; carers are less likely to be in work, and to work shorter hours when they are in work; furthermore, they may have lower hourly rates of pay (Joshi, 1994). Parker and Lawton (1990) found that carers earned an average £8 per week less than non carers, the difference being £16 per week for men, and £4 per week for women (1985 prices).

Table 7 shows weekly net personal income for men and women from all sources.[3] The findings confirm Parker and Lawton's analysis of the GHS, with retired male past carers having a mean weekly income of £13 less than non carers, and non-retired male past carers having a mean weekly income of £16 less than non-carers (1988/9 prices). Only the difference between retired carers and non carers was significant at the 90% confidence level. Median weekly incomes, which are less affected by extreme incomes, are much lower, and the differences between carers and non-carers are small and not statistically significant.

3 Total personal income is created from the sum of all income (earned income, pension income, investment income, state benefits, and any other income, less tax paid direct to the Inland Revenue). Of nearly 3,000 cases where total income could be computed, there were two cases where total income exceeded £7,000 per week. Since these amounts seemed implausible, and as means, standard errors and tests of significance are strongly influenced by extreme numbers, these two cases were not included in the analysis.

Table 7: Weekly personal income (£s); by gender, carer and retirement status

| | Men | | | | | |
| | Retired | | | Non-retired | | |
	Median (£s pw)	Mean (£s pw)	N	Median (£s pw)	Mean (£s pw)	N
Past carers	76.22 (1.9)[4]	96.29 (5.0)	176	130.00 (3.3)	138.27 (7.7)	132
Non-carers	80.79 (1.9)	109.03 (5.5)	397	132.89 (2.3)	154.74 (6.6)	416
	Women					
	Retired			Non-retired		
Past carers	44.59 (0.8)	55.82 (2.3)	432	63.12 (1.9)	70.83 (4.5)	192
Non-carers	40.83 (0.6)	42.47 (1.8)	388	62.84 (1.7)	73.52 (4.3)	159

Source: Retirement Survey, Great Britain, 1988

Figure 1: Mean weekly income (£s) by gender, carer and retirement status

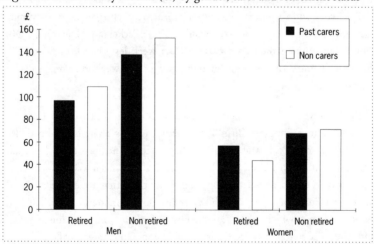

For women, however, the picture is rather different (Figure 1). Retired women past carers had a weekly mean income of £13 (±£5)[5] per week *more* than non carers, a difference of nearly 25%. There are a number of possible

---

[4] In all tables figures in brackets are standard errors.

[5] 90% confidence intervals unles otherwise stated.

Table 8: Average weekly personal income (£s) of past carers; by gender and retirement status, people caring for fewer or more than ten years

	Men					
	Retired			Non-retired		
	Median (£s pw)	Mean (£s pw)	N	Median (£s pw)	Mean (£s pw)	N
<10 years	77.75 (2.6)	98.10 (6.2)	125	139.76 (4.1)	144.17 (8.8)	97
>10 years	71.92 (4.2)	91.31 (8.0)	51	118.98 (8.6)	122.82 (15.7)	35
	Women					
	Retired			Non-retired		
<10 years	45.18 (1.1)	59.35 (3.0)	296	67.45 (2.4)	77.54 (5.5)	120
>10 years	42.74 (1.3)	48.00 (3.0)	136	41.71 (3.5)	49.97 (6.2)	39

Source: Retirement Survey, Great Britain, 1988

explanations for this. For example, more past carers were widows and could therefore have inherited their husbands' pensions. Median weekly incomes were lower, with a difference of only £4 a week. For non-retired women the differences between the incomes of past carers and non-carers were small and subject to wide margins of error.

Different carer subgroups show very interesting differentials in the amounts of total personal income, with those who had cared for more than ten years having considerably less income than those who had cared for fewer than ten years. This was true for both men and women, retired or not retired. The differences must be regarded as suggestive only, as the sample sizes are small. For men, the differences are all subject to wide margins of error. The most robust finding is the gap of £21 difference between the median incomes of non-retired "long" and "short" term carers. The median income of non-retired past carers who had been carers for more than ten years was £21 below that of non-retired past carers whose caring had not lasted so long, although even this figure has a margin of error of ±£16.

For women, the differences are proportionately greater, and for both retired and non retired women are significant at the 99% confidence level. Retired women who had cared for more than ten years had mean incomes of £11 lower than women who had cared for fewer than ten years, and non retired

Table 9: Weekly personal income (£s) of past carers; by gender and retirement status, people reporting no effect/any effect on their working lives

	Men					
	Retired			Non-retired		
	Median (£s pw)	Mean (£s pw)	N	Median (£s pw)	Mean (£s pw)	N
No effect	76.22 (2.1)	96.36 (5.2)	150	130.29 (3.6)	141.20 (8.3)	120
Effect	75.83 (8.2)	95.93 (15.7)	26	–	–	12
	Women					
	Retired			Non-retired		
No effect	44.86 (1.0)	57.51 (2.8)	316	65.38 (2.5)	75.28 (5.7)	117
Effect	44.10 (1.5)	51.25 (3.5)	116	58.16 (3.1)	60.00 (6.1)	42

Source: Retirement Survey, Great Britain, 1988

women who had cared for more than ten years had incomes of £28 per week lower than their counterparts who had cared for fewer than ten years. This represents an average income of around three fifths of the income of non retired women who had cared for fewer than ten years, and of the income of non carers.

There are also differences, although they are generally not as pronounced, according to whether or not people reported an effect of caring on their working lives,[6] with the incomes of those reporting an effect consistently lower than those not reporting an effect. However, sample sizes are now very small so the differences are generally not statistically significant. The only exception is for non-retired women, where the differences are just significant at the 90% level.

Earnings
Past carers who were still in employment at the time of the survey had lower incomes from that employment than people who had never cared (Table 10).

---

[6] People reporting at least one of the following effects: lost job and became unemployed, took lower paid job, had difficulty getting a job, lost pay because of shorter hours. See Table 6 above.

Table 10: Weekly income from employment (£s) of people who were working in the previous week; by gender and carer status

	Men		
	Median (£s pw)	Mean (£s pw)	N
Past carers	120.75 (3.0)	122.62 (7.0)	150
Non-carers	124.44 (2.0)	140.28 (6.0)	474
	Women		
Past carers	42.00 (1.7)	58.92 (4.2)	182
Non-carers	54.54 (1.7)	66.54 (4.2)	186

Source: Retirement Survey, Great Britain, 1988

The gap was clearest for the median incomes of women where there was a difference of £13 (±£4) or 30% (±7%). Male past carers had mean incomes from employment which were 14% (±10%) of the level of non carers – a difference of £18 (±£15) per week.

Figure 2: Mean weekly income from employment (£s) of people working in the past week: non carers, people caring for fewer and more than ten years

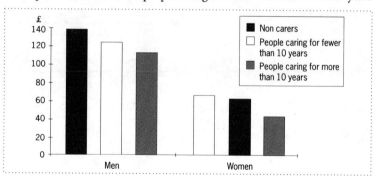

Past carers who were in employment and had cared for more than ten years were considerably worse off than other past carers (Table 11 and Figure 2).

Although margins of error are wide, the difference for women, at least, is noteworthy. The median income of women who had spent more than 10 years caring was £20 (±£6) below that for women whose caring had not lasted so long – a shortfall of 40%.

Table 11: Weekly income from employment (£s) of past carers who were working in the previous week; by gender, people caring for fewer and more than ten years

	Men		
	Median (£s pw)	Mean (£s pw)	N
<10 years	121.52 (3.7)	124.67 (8.3)	106
>10 years	113.22 (7.4)	117.27 (13.3)	44
	Women		
<10 years	50.24 (2.2)	64.66 (5.2)	132
>10 years	30.00 (3.3)	42.53 (6.2)	50

Source: Retirement Survey, Great Britain, 1988

Table 12: Weekly income from employment (£s) of past carers who were working in the previous week; by gender, people reporting effect/no effect on working lives

	Men		
	Median (£s pw)	Mean (£s pw)	N
No effect	118.46 (3.2)	122.61 (7.5)	140
Effect	–	–	10
	Women		
	Median (£s pw)	Mean (£s pw)	N
No effect	47.03 (2.2)	62.59 (5.0)	138
Effect	36.53 (3.6)	48.61 (7.1)	44

Source: Retirement Survey, Great Britain, 1988

Women past carers whose working lives had been affected by their caring responsibilities tended to have lower incomes than those reporting no such effect (Table 12). The gap between their median incomes was £11 (±£7). For men the differences were small, however, and statistically insignificant.

Occupational and private pensions

Evidence on the effect that past caring has had on pension income is presented in Table 13. There was little difference in the proportions of past carers and non-carers who had some income from occupational or private pensions. Almost two-thirds of retired men and between a fifth and a quarter of retired women had a pension from a previous employer or from their own contributions into a private pension scheme. The difference in the mean amounts for past carers and non-carers were very small for men. For women the average pensions of past carers were actually £3 per week higher than for non-carers but with a margin of error of ±£2. Although not large, this difference may reflect differences in the types of women who choose, or are able to take on caring, rather than the effects of caring. For example, single women may be more likely to have earned themselves an occupational pension and more likely to have been carers than married women.

Table 13: Average weekly income from occupational and private pensions (own account); by gender, retirement and carer status

	Men					
	Retired			Non-retired		
	Mean (£s pw)	% with any*	N	Mean (£s pw)	% with any	N
Past carers	38.71 (3.6)	65	225	7.34 (2.1)	15	151
Non-carers	40.95 (2.9)	66	458	7.99 (1.1)	16	512
	Women					
	Retired			Non-retired		
	Mean (£s pw)	% with any*	N	Mean (£s pw)	% with any	N
Past carers	8.19 (1.0)	24	516	1.56 (0.7)	7	200
Non-carers	5.55 (0.7)	22	462	0.98 (0.5)	4	228

Source: Retirement Survey, Great Britain, 1988
* % who have any income from occupational or private pension on own (not spouse's) account.

Not surprisingly, relatively few non-retired people had income from occupational and private pensions, although, for men the income did amount to
£8 a week on average. Differences in the pension income of past and non-
carers who were not retired were small.

As so few non-retired people had income from occupational or private
pensions, Tables 14 and 15 examine the incomes of only retired past carers.
There are no clear differences between men and women who cared for fewer
or more than ten years. However retired men who reported that caring had
no effect on their working lives had incomes from occupational and private
pensions almost three times as high as retired men who reported an effect.
The gap in their average pension income amounted to £27, albeit with a
fairly wide margin of error of ±£11. The median pension income of those
reporting an effect was £20 (±£5) lower than that of men who reported no
effect. The corresponding differences for women were small and not
statistically significant.

Table 14: Average weekly income from occupational and private pensions
(own account) of retired past carers; by gender, people caring for fewer or
more than ten years

	Men		
	Mean (£s pw)	% with any	N
<10 years	39.74 (4.3)	68	163
>10 years	35.92 (6.3)	60	67
	Women		
	Mean (£s pw)	% with any	N
<10 years	8.50 (1.1)	27	351
>10 years	7.56 (2.1)	20	168

Source: Retirement Survey, Great Britain, 1988

Table 15: Average weekly income from occupational and private pensions (own account) of retired past carers; by gender, people reporting effect/no effect on working lives

	Men		
	Mean (£s pw)	% with any	N
No effect	43.42 (4.0)	72	194
Effect	16.73 (5.6)	38	36
	Women		
	Mean (£s pw)	% with any	N
No effect	8.99 (1.3)	26	386
Effect	5.85 (1.5)	20	133

Source: Retirement Survey, Great Britain, 1988

Savings income

Investment income can supplement or replace earnings and pensions. Parker and Lawton (1990) found little evidence that this had happened for carers in the 1985 GHS, with other income playing virtually no role in boosting overall income for women, and modifying the original earnings gap of £16 per week between male carers and non-carers by only £4 (Parker and Lawton, 1990:19). They also found that the people providing the most intensive levels of care were substantially less likely that their non-carer equivalents to have any income from their savings. Parker and Lawton concluded that this is a real, and important, effect of care-giving.

In theory, however, it is possible that past carers, especially those who have dedicated large portions of their lives to caring, have capital from inheritances which do substitute for lost earnings and pensions.

There is some evidence for this from Table 16, which compares the investment income of past carers and non-carers, standardising for gender and retirement status. Both male and female retired carers have higher mean weekly incomes from their investments than people who had never cared. In both cases, larger proportions actually had any investment income; three-quarters of retired male carers had investment income, compared with a little more than three-fifths of retired non-carers. Smaller proportions of women

Table 16: Weekly investment income; by gender, carer and retirement status

	Men					
	Retired			Non-retired		
	Mean (£s pw)	% with any	N	Mean (£s pw)	% with any	N
Past carers	15.43 (2.7)	75	181	8.06 (3.0)	70	132
Non-carers	10.42 (1.2)	62	407	6.67 (1.2)	62	422
	Women					
	Retired			Non-retired		
	Mean (£s pw)	% with any	N	Mean (£s pw)	% with any	N
Past carers	9.31 (1.3)	66	436	10.54 (2.8)	58	160
Non-carers	6.67 (0.9)	61	396	7.30 (1.6)	66	195

Source: Retirement Survey, Great Britain, 1988

actually had investment income, but again past carers tended to have higher levels of savings than the non-carers. The differences in investment income are statistically significant for retired men (95% confidence level) and for retired women (90% confidence level). For non-retired men and women, the differences are not statistically significant. The means are heavily influenced by a handful of people with very large investment incomes, and the medians are much lower, at around £3 a week for retired male past carers, and less than £1 a week for their female equivalents.

Table 17 shows that there is considerable variation between sub-groups of carers, with those who had cared for more than ten years earning much less in investment income than their counterparts who had cared for fewer than ten years. Amongst retired men who had cared for fewer than ten years, the large majority – nearly 80% – had investment income of some kind, with a mean weekly income of £17. This is £6 more than the mean investment income of carers who had cared for ten years or more, and the proportion having any investment income at all was also lower, with only two-thirds having such income. The differentials are not as pronounced for retired women, with similar proportions having investment income of any kind, and a mean

Table 17: Weekly investment income of past carers; by gender and retirement status, people caring for fewer or more than ten years

	Men					
	Retired			Non-retired		
	Mean (£s pw)	% with any	N	Mean (£s pw)	% with any	N
<10 years	17.06 (3.5)	78	128	9.41 (4.0)	72	97
>10 years	11.02 (3.5)	64	53	4.55 (1.4)	63	35
	Women					
	Retired			Non-retired		
	Mean (£s pw)	% with any	N	Mean (£s pw)	% with any	N
<10 years	10.35 (1.7)	65	297	12.45 (3.7)	58	120
>10 years	7.03 (1.4)	68	139	4.52 (1.3)	59	40

Source: Retirement Survey, Great Britain, 1988

weekly income difference of around £3. There were larger differences, however, of nearly £8 per week, between non-retired women who had cared for fewer than and more than ten years. Although the figures in this table suggest that people providing care for extended periods are substantially less likely to have investment income than people who had provided care for shorter periods, the sample sizes are so small, and the standard errors so large, that it is impossible to be sure.

Women who reported at least one effect of caring on their working lives had lower levels of investment income than those who reported no effect (Table 18). Amongst the retired the gap was £6 (±£3) and amongst the non-retired it was £11 (±£6). For men the reverse appears to be true, although sample sizes are too small to draw firm conclusions.

Table 18: Average weekly investment income of past carers; by gender and retirement status, people reporting no effect/any effect on their working lives

	Men					
	Retired			Non-retired		
	Mean (£s pw)	% with any	N	Mean (£s pw)	% with any	N
No effect	13.45 (2.8)	80	152	8.63 (3.2)	71	120
Effect	23.97 (8.5)	53	29	–	–	12
	Women					
	Retired			Non-retired		
	Mean (£s pw)	% with any	N	Mean (£s pw)	% with any	N
No effect	10.88 (1.6)	70	320	13.78 (3.8)	64	118
Effect	4.98 (1.2)	56	116	2.56 (1.2)	45	42

Source: Retirement Survey, Great Britain, 1988

State benefits

We now turn to a consideration of the receipt of state benefits by past carers and non-carers. We begin with the State Pension before going on to look at other income from the state. Tables 19, 20 and 21 describe the levels of state retirement and widow's pension received by retired past carers and non-carers who were over state pension age. There is not a great deal of evidence that caring responsibilities lead to lower levels of state pension. In general, differences between the pensions of past carers and non-carers, of those caring for more than ten years and those who had cared for shorter periods, and of those reporting an effect on their working lives and those reporting no effect were small and not statistically significant. There were two noticeable exceptions. The median state pension income of women who had cared for more than ten years was unambiguously and substantially lower than those who had cared for shorter periods. The gap was £9 a week with a margin of error of just £1. In contrast, the median state pension of women reporting an effect of caring on their working lives was £16 (±£1) *higher* than that of women who reported no such effect. One interpretation of this is that it is only those with a relatively strong attachment to the labour market and who

Table 19: Weekly income from state retirement and widow's pension; retired people over state pension age, by gender and carer status

	Men			
	Median (£s pw)	Mean (£s pw)	% with any	N
Past carers	45.03 (0.6)	44.08 (1.3)	93	137
Non-carers	44.19 (0.5)	38.68 (1.3)	82	257
	Women			
	Median (£s pw)	Mean (£s pw)	% with any	N
Past carers	29.66 (0.3)	30.75 (0.8)	91	444
Non-carers	25.01 (0.3)	26.67 (0.8)	87	386

Source: Retirement Survey, Great Britain, 1988

Table 20: Weekly income from state retirement and widow's pension; retired people over state pension age, by gender, people caring for fewer or more than 10 years

	Men			
	Median (£s pw)	Mean (£s pw)	% with any	N
<10 years	45.35 (0.7)	44.01 (1.6)	93	96
>10 years	44.72 (1.3)	44.25 (2.2)	93	41
	Women			
	Median (£s pw)	Mean (£s pw)	% with any	N
<10 years	34.83 (0.4)	31.14 (0.9)	92	292
>10 years	26.30 (0.5)	29.97 (1.2)	89	152

Source: Retirement Survey, Great Britain, 1988

Table 21: Weekly income from state retirement and widow's pension; retired people over state pension age, by gender, people reporting no effect/any effect on working life

	Men			
	Median (£s pw)	Mean (£s pw)	% with any	N
No effect	45.14 (0.6)	44.57 (1.4)	93	114
Effect	44.62 (1.8)	41.42 (2.8)	91	23
	Women			
	Median (£s pw)	Mean (£s pw)	% with any	N
No effect	25.61 (0.3)	29.78 (0.9)	90	325
Effect	41.39 (0.6)	33.39 (1.4)	94	119

Source: Retirement Survey, Great Britain, 1988

Table 22: Average weekly income from all state benefits except retirement/widow's pension; by gender, carer and retirement status

	Men					
	Retired			Non-retired		
	Mean (£s pw)	% with any	N	Mean (£s pw)	% with any	N
Past carer	15.47 (1.9)	27	227	7.67 (1.5)	17	152
Non-carer	24.37 (1.6)	40	472	8.34 (1.0)	15	511
	Women					
	Retired			Non-retired		
	Mean (£s pw)	% with any	N	Mean (£s pw)	% with any	N
Past carer	5.04 (0.6)	18	515	2.17 (0.6)	8	202
Non-carer	3.69 (0.6)	13	466	2.28 (0.6)	9	225

Source: Retirement Survey, Great Britain, 1988

have therefore earned themselves a state pension in their own right who report such effects.

It is only amongst retired men that there appears to be much difference in the levels of other state benefits received by past carers and non-carers (Table 22). At £15 a week, past carers received £9 (±£4) a week *less* than non-carers on average.[7] This difference arises mainly because a larger proportion of non-carers received any state benefits (other than retirement/widow's pension); 40% received some income from these benefits compared with only 27% for past carers. Women received lower amounts of these state benefits than men – partly because in the case of couples, benefits such as Income Support are generally paid to the man – and with only small differences between past carers and non-carers.

Once we look at subgroups of carers (Tables 23 and 24), differences are a little more apparent. Only a quarter of retired men who had cared for fewer

Table 23: Average income from all state benefits except retirement/widow's pensions, of past carers; by gender and retirement status, people caring for fewer or more than ten years

	Men					
	Retired			Non-retired		
	Mean (£s pw)	% with any	N	Mean (£s pw)	% with any	N
<10 years	15.22 (2.3)	25	160	6.75 (1.7)	17	108
>10 years	16.14 (3.3)	31	67	9.84 (3.2)	19	44
	Women					
	Retired			Non-retired		
	Mean (£s pw)	% with any	N	Mean (£s pw)	% with any	N
<10 years	5.50 (0.8)	18	349	2.23 (0.7)	9	146
>10 years	4.07 (0.9)	16	166	2.02 (1.2)	5	56

Source: Retirement Survey, Great Britain, 1988

[7] In all cases the median incomes from these benefits were zero, because of the large proportions not receiving any income at all from this source.

Table 24: Average income from all state benefits, except state retirement/ widow's pensions, of past carers; by gender and retirement status, people reporting effect/no effect on their working lives

	Men					
	Retired			Non-retired		
	Mean (£s pw)	% with any	N	Mean (£s pw)	% with any	N
No effect	12.78 (1.8)	23	193	6.84 (1.5)	15	138
Effect	28.49 (6.8)	45	34	–	–	14

	Women					
	Retired			Non-retired		
	Mean (£s pw)	% with any	N	Mean (£s pw)	% with any	N
No effect	4.56 (0.7)	16	382	1.65 (0.6)	7	150
Effect	6.44 (1.4)	22	133	3.51 (1.6)	10	52

Source: Retirement Survey, Great Britain, 1988

than ten years had any income from state benefits, apart from the state pension, compared with 31% of those who had cared for more than ten years. Even so, differences in the average amounts were small. Male past carers who reported an effect of caring on their working lives had considerably higher income from these benefits than men who reported no effect on their working lives. Retired male past carers who reported an effect on their working lives had mean incomes from benefits more than twice as high as men who reported no effect, differences which are statistically significant. Women reporting an effect also had higher incomes from benefits, although the actual levels and the proportional differences are much smaller and not statistically significant.

FAMILY INCOME

Although we have found that the personal incomes of carers, and of certain subgroups of carers in particular, are low, it is possible that they are moderated by access to household incomes that are reasonably prosperous. Whether all household/family members share equally in household/family income is the subject of much debate. However the general picture to emerge from secondary analyses of the General Household Survey and the Disability

Survey (Baldwin and Parker, 1991; Martin and White, 1988; Matthews and Truscott, 1990) is that households containing both disabled people and carers have lower incomes than similar households in the general population.

The magnitude of the difference is strongly influenced by household size, and carer-type. Parker and Lawton (1994) controlled for this using per capita household income (total household income divided by the number of people, including dependent children, in the household), and by using an equivalent income scale (the Luxembourg Income Scale, consisting of 1 for the first person in the household and 0.5 for each subsequent adult or child, to calculate equivalent incomes). Using the latter, Parker and Lawton found few differences between the incomes of carers and non carers. The per capita income comparison, however, revealed that the household income of carers was significantly lower than that of equivalent non carers. Where the most intensive forms of care were needed, or the household contained a co-resident carer, there were differences in income of £15 and £14 per week respectively (Parker and Lawton, 1990).

Evidence on current carers' incomes suggests, therefore, that carers are not well-off themselves, and do not live in well-off households, although the method by which household size is taken into account may be important.

Income levels
The figures in Table 25 compare the total benefit unit income of past carers and non-carers. Table 26 compares past carers according to whether they had cared for fewer than or more than ten years, and Table 27 by whether they reported an effect on their working life. Here the income of all members of the benefit unit[8] in which the past carer or non-carer lives has been totalled and ascribed to each adult living in the unit. A benefit unit consists of a single person, or a couple, and their dependent children. Income has been equivalised using the OECD scale of 1 for the first adult, 0.7 for each subsequent adult or child aged at least 14 years, and 0.5 for each younger child.

There is some indication that retired men who had been carers had lower family incomes than their non-carer counterparts. The median family income of retired male past carers was £5 (±£3) per week lower than that of retired men who had not been carers. The gap between their average family incomes was £4 a week but with a margin of error of ±£9. Evidence of lower family incomes amongst non-retired male past carers is not strong; their median income was in fact higher, by £6 (±£4) a week than that of non-carers although their average income was £8 (±£11) a week lower than non-carers.

---

[8] It is not possible to construct household income since in the Retirement Survey it is only the respondent and spouse for whom income information was collected.

Amongst retired women, the family incomes of past carers seem to have been higher than those of non-carers, which is what has already been found for personal incomes. The average family income of retired female past carers was £8 (±£6) a week higher than non-carers and their median income £4 (±£2) a week higher. The situation was reversed amongst non-retired women where both mean and median incomes were higher for non-carers than for past carers, but not by statistically significant amounts.

Comparing past carers who had cared for fewer than and more than ten years, differences in family incomes follow a similar pattern to personal incomes. In all cases, average and median family incomes were lower for people who had cared for more than ten years than for past carers whose caring had lasted for shorter periods.

Figure 3: Mean weekly benefit unit income (£s): non carers, people caring for fewer and more than ten years

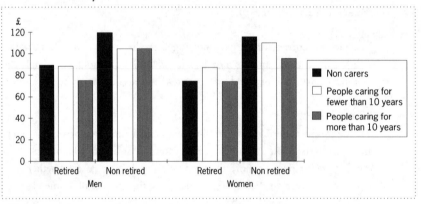

Although differences in mean incomes were not statistically significant, differences in median incomes were; and were greater for the non-retired than the retired. The median income of non-retired men who had cared for more than ten years was £16 (±£12) a week lower than for those whose period of caring had been shorter; for women the equivalent gap was £19 (±£11).

Finally, a comparison between past carers who reported any effect and no effect of caring on their employment suggests lower family incomes amongst those who reported an effect. Although not generally statistically significant for men, differences in mean and median incomes were statistically significant for women and were again larger amongst the non-retired. Both mean and median incomes of non-retired female past carers were about £30 lower for those whose working lives had been affected by their caring responsibilities than for those reporting no such effect.

Table 25: Weekly equivalent net benefit unit income; by gender, carer and retirement status

	Men					
	Retired			Non-retired		
	Median (£s pw)	Mean (£s pw)	N	Median (£s pw)	Mean (£s pw)	N
Past carers	66.08 (1.6)	85.54 (4.0)	174	111.73 (2.3)	111.59 (5.3)	123
Non-carers	70.81 (1.4)	89.91 (4.1)	387	105.92 (1.5)	119.56 (4.3)	394
	Women					
	Retired			Non-retired		
	Median (£s pw)	Mean (£s pw)	N	Median (£s pw)	Mean (£s pw)	N
Past carers	63.93 (1.0)	83.88 (3.0)	421	99.99 (2.1)	107.79 (5.0)	148
Non-carers	60.43 (0.9)	75.84 (2.5)	377	101.90 (5.4)	116.41 (0.9)	181

Source: Retirement Survey, Great Britain, 1988

Table 26: Weekly equivalent net benefit unit income, past carers; by gender and retirement status, people caring for fewer/more than ten years

	Men					
	Retired			Non-retired		
	Median (£s pw)	Mean (£s pw)	N	Median (£s pw)	Mean (£s pw)	N
<10 years	67.72 (2.1)	88.70 (5.2)	123	117.07 (2.7)	113.89 (5.7)	89
>10 years	58.57 (3.0)	76.99 (5.7)	51	100.64 (6.6)	105.88 (12.1)	34
	Women					
	Retired			Non-retired		
	Median (£s pw)	Mean (£s pw)	N	Median (£s pw)	Mean (£s pw)	N
<10 years	66.31 (1.2)	87.41 (3.4)	289	101.00 (2.4)	110.63 (5.5)	112
>10 years	59.68 (2.6)	75.99 (6.1)	132	81.81 (6.6)	98.44 (11.6)	36

Source: Retirement Survey, Great Britain, 1988

Table 27: Weekly equivalent net benefit unit income of past carers; by gender and retirement status, people reporting no effect/any effect on working lives

	Men					
	Retired			Non-retired		
	Median (£s pw)	Mean (£s pw)	N	Median (£s pw)	Mean (£s pw)	N
No effect	68.29 (1.6)	86.57 (4.0)	148	113.14 (2.4)	113.85 (5.5)	113
Effect	54.74 (7.8)	80.87 (15.0)	26	–	–	10
	Women					
	Retired			Non-retired		
	Median (£s pw)	Mean (£s pw)	N	Median (£s pw)	Mean (£s pw)	N
No effect	68.25 (1.1)	85.86 (3.2)	309	109.73 (2.7)	116.35 (6.0)	109
Effect	56.38 (3.2)	78.42 (7.2)	112	78.90 (4.2)	87.10 (8.1)	39

Source: Retirement Survey, Great Britain, 1988

Receipt of means-tested benefits

A possible consequence of caring is a greater reliance on means-tested benefits. Reduced employment and earnings prospects may result in earnings which fall below the level at which Income Support and Housing Benefit become payable before retirement and cause lower pensions and therefore entitlement to these benefits during retirement. Table 28 shows what proportion of past carers and non-carers were living in families receiving Income Support and/ or Housing Benefit.

A very consistent picture emerges. For men and women, retired and non-retired, the proportion receiving means-tested benefits is higher for past carers than non-carers; for 'long-term' than for 'short-term' carers; and for those reporting an effect of caring on their working lives than for those stating no effect. The differences are not all statistically significant. In particular, as we have found elsewhere, the differences between all past carers and non-carers are subject to the greatest uncertainty. It is only amongst retired men that the 90% confidence interval for difference in the proportions receiving means-tested benefits implies an unambiguously higher proportion amongst those caring for more than ten years. However, the

Table 28: Receipt of means-tested state benefits; by gender and retirement status

	Men			
	Retired		Non-retired	
	% receiving IS/HB*	N	% receiving IS/HB*	N
Past carers	31	228	10	152
Non-carers	27	474	9	513
<10 years caring	26	162	7	108
>10 years caring	42	66	17	44
No effect of caring on working lives	27	194	9	138
Any effect of caring on working lives	49	34	–	14
	Women			
	Retired		Non-retired	
	% receiving IS/HB*	N	% receiving IS/HB*	N
Past carers	33	516	17	202
Non-carers	30	467	11	230
<10 years caring	32	349	17	146
>10 years caring	35	167	16	56
No effect of caring on working lives	29	383	12	150
Any effect of caring on working lives	45	133	29	52

Source: Retirement Survey, Great Britain, 1988
*Income Support and/or Housing Benefit

strongest difference is between those reporting any effect and no effect on their working lives. Here all differences are statistically significant except amongst non-retired men where the sample reporting an effect is only 14. In each other case those past carers who reported an effect of caring on their employment were unambiguously more likely to be in receipt of Income Support and/or Housing Benefit.

SUMMARY

The finding which stands out most clearly from the analysis of past carers' current incomes is that people who had cared for more than ten years had which were lower than those who had cared for shorter periods of time and lower than the incomes of non-carers. This applied to their personal incomes, their family incomes and to the earnings of those who were in paid work. It applied to men and women alike, and to the retired and non-retired. People who had been carers for more than ten years were also more likely to be dependent on means-tested state benefits. Research on current carers has shown the importance of distinguishing between those for whom caring takes up many hours a week and those who provide lower levels of care. The corresponding finding from our analysis is the distinction between carers who have devoted many years to caring and those for whom caring lasted for shorter periods. We cannot say from our data whether the two – long hours and long years – go hand-in-hand.

There are some surprises in the findings. In the first place, retired women who were past-carers had higher incomes than retired women who had not been carers. This appears to be due, at least in part, to higher incomes from their own occupational and private pensions. There are a number of possible explanations for this. Importantly, it may say more about the kinds of women who *become* carers than it does about the *effects* of caring. Another surprising finding is that past-carers had higher incomes from savings than non-carers. Again we can only speculate about the explanations for this. One possibility, given that past-carers were more likely to be widowed than non-carers, is that they have inherited capital from a deceased spouse.

In keeping with existing research on current carers, we find that differences between past carers as a single group and non carers were not great. An exception was the gap between the earnings of employed past carers and non-carers: the average and median earnings of past carers were lower than those of non-carers and the differences were especially marked for women.

Differences between the personal incomes, and to a lesser extent the family incomes, of men and women far outweighed differences between past carers and non-carers. Thus men who were past carers had personal incomes which were higher than women non-carers; men who had cared for more than ten years had incomes which were greater than women who had cared for fewer than ten years; and men who reported that caring had had an effect on their working lives had incomes well above those of women who reported no such effect. Similar comparisons can be drawn for every component of income.

However, caring does seem to have effects on income even after caring ceases, although the effects are varied, with the single most important factor appearing to be the length of time a past carer has devoted to caring.

4. THE EFFECT OF CARING ON EMPLOYMENT AND PENSION HISTORIES

EMPLOYMENT

The effect that caring responsibilities have on concurrent employment patterns has received considerable attention (see for example, Parker and Lawton, 1990, Evandrou and Winter, 1992). The longer-term consequences are less well known. There are a number of ways in which caring may affect participation in paid work even after caring has ceased. Where caring has reduced earnings, curtailed the accumulation of pensions rights or raised living costs, there will be an increased financial incentive to take on work once caring ceases. On the other hand the wage rate past carers can command might have been lowered by absence from the labour market so there may also be a reduced incentive to participate in paid work. In addition, non-financial costs and benefits of working after caring – such as the social benefits of going out to work – may come into play. In this section we explore the patterns of current and past employment amongst past carers to investigate the balance of these factors.

Current employment patterns amongst past carers and non-carers

Amongst men aged 55 to 59 and men aged 65 to 69, past carers were considerably less likely than non-carers to have a paid job at the time of the Retirement Survey. Over 70% of men aged 55–59 who had never been a carer were in paid work compared with just 60% of past carers in the same age group (Table 29). Once state pension age was reached non-carers were twice as likely as past carers to have a job. In the intervening age groups the proportions of non-carers and past carers who were in work were similar:

Table 29: Proportions of past carers and non-carers in paid work; by gender and age

	Men aged:		
	55–59	60–64	65–69
Past carers (%)	60	53	6
N (base)	114	125	143
Non-carers (%)	72	51	13
N (base)	356	347	286
	Women aged:		
	55–59	60–64	65–69
Past carers (%)	51	22	9
N (base)	193	247	281
Non carers (%)	53	19	6
N (base)	231	263	204

Source: Retirement Survey, Great Britain, 1988

slightly more than half in both cases. The differences between non-carers and past carers were less pronounced for women but past carers were *more* likely to be working beyond state pension age. There is thus some evidence, perhaps, that women attempt to make up for lost time once caring ceases.

Amongst those who did have jobs, there were noticeable differences in the hours worked by non-carers and past carers (Tables 30 and 31). Higher proportions of past carers worked for fewer than 20 hours a week while lower proportions worked for 30 or more hours. Almost 9 out of 10 men aged 60–64 who had never had caring responsibilities worked for 30 or more hours a week, compared with 1 in 2 past carers in the same age group. The proportions of women past carers working fewer than 20 hours a week was high: over a third in the 55–59 age group and more than a half in the 60–64 age group.

Table 30: Weekly hours worked; by age and carer status, men in paid work

	Men aged:	
	55–59	60–64
Past carers working:		
< 20 hours (%)	4	13
20–29 hours (%)	3	4
30+ hours (%)	94	50
N (base)	74	69
Non-carers working:		
< 20 hours (%)	1	7
20–29 hours (%)	2	4
30+ hours (%)	96	89
N (base)	263	175

Source: Retirement Survey, Great Britain, 1988

Table 31: Weekly hours worked; by age and carer status, women in paid work

	Women aged:	
	55–59	60–64
Past carers working:		
< 20 hours (%)	35	56
20–29 hours (%)	19	18
30+ hours (%)	45	26
N (base)	103	53
Non-carers working:		
< 20 hours (%)	26	36
20–29 hours (%)	27	31
30+ hours (%)	47	32
N (base)	123	49

Source: Retirement Survey, Great Britain, 1988

Overall, therefore, men who were past carers tended to be less likely to be in a paid job than non-carers and if they did have a job, tended to work fewer hours. Beyond state pension age, women who were past carers were, if anything, more likely to be in paid work than non-carers but again if they did have a job, they generally worked fewer hours.

Employment histories of past carers and non-carers

One indicator of the long-term consequences of caring is the proportion of adult life spent in paid employment. This is what is shown in Table 32 for non-carers and past carers. Adult life is defined as the time which has elapsed since reaching the age of 16. For men the average proportion of adult life

Table 32: Proportions of adult life spent in paid work; by gender and age

	Men aged:		
	55–59	60–64	65–69
Mean % of adult life in full-time work			
Past carers (%)	94	92	90
	(1.2)	(1.4)	(0.8)
N	114	125	143
Non-carers (%)	94	93	87
	(0.1)	(0.7)	(0.8)
N	356	347	286
	Women aged:		
	55–59	60–64	65–69
Mean % of adult life in full-time work			
Past carers (%)	43	41	39
	(2.1)	(1.6)	(1.5)
N	193	246	281
Non carers (%)	45	38	34
	(1.8)	(1.5)	(1.7)
N	231	263	204
Mean % of adult life in part-time work			
Past-carers (%)	24	22	14
	(1.7)	(1.3)	(1.2)
N	193	247	281
Non-carers (%)	19	17	14
	(1.4)	(1.2)	(1.0)
N	231	263	204

Source: Retirement Survey, Great Britain, 1988

spent in full-time work is shown and we can see that there was not a great deal of difference between the figures for non-carers and past carers. Only in the oldest age group had past carers spent noticeably lower proportions of their adult life in paid work and even here the difference is small: 87% compared with 90%. This pattern is consistent with our finding that men who were past carers were markedly less likely to be in paid work beyond state pension age than non-carers. For women it is interesting to draw comparisons for part-time as well as full-time work. Differences between past carers and non-carers are again small but past carers in the 60–64 and 65–69 age groups had spent greater proportions of their lives in full-time paid work than non-carers. Those in the 55–59 and 60–64 age groups had spent greater proportions of time in part-time work, on average.

Table 33: Proportion of adult life spent in paid work; by age and gender, people caring for fewer or more than ten years

	Men aged:		
	55–59	60–64	65–69
Mean % of adult life in full-time work			
< 10 years (%)	94	91	91
	(1.5)	(1.7)	(1.0)
N	82	88	101
> 10 years (%)	94	92	88
	(0.8)	(2.5)	(1.6)
N	32	37	42
	Women aged:		
	55–59	60–64	65–69
Mean % of adult life in full-time work			
< 10 years (%)	44	43	39
	(2.4)	(2.0)	(1.9)
N	143	170	183
> 10 years (%)	38	35	38
	(3.8)	(2.6)	(2.6)
N	50	76	98
Mean % of adult life in part-time work			
< 10 years (%)	23	22	12
	(2.0)	(1.6)	(1.2)
N	143	171	183
> 10 years (%)	25	21	18
	(3.6)	(2.3)	(2.2)
N	50	76	98

Source: Retirement Survey, Great Britain, 1988

Distinguishing those who have spent fewer than and more than ten years caring for someone, indicates that at least amongst women, those caring for longer periods had not spent as much time in full-time work (Table 33). The difference was most noticeable amongst the youngest age group who might be expected to have had less time to catch up. Proportions of adult life that women spent in part time work were similar for those who had cared for fewer than and more than ten years.

Employment patterns before, during and after caring

Our principle objective is to examine what happens to carers once they cease caring. We therefore turn now to a consideration of how much of the time

Table 34: Proportion of adult life spent in paid work before, during and after caring; by age and gender

	Men aged:		
	55–59	60–64	65–69
Mean % of adult life in full-time work			
Prior to caring	100	98	100
	(2.0)	(1.5)	(0.9)
During caring	86	83	79
	(3.1)	(3.1)	(3.1)
After caring	70	65	45
	(4.1)	(3.6)	(3.2)
N	105	119	138
	Women aged:		
	55–59	60–64	65–69
Mean % of adult life in full-time work			
Prior to caring	59	60	55
	(3.7)	(2.2)	(2.0)
During Caring	25	22	25
	(3.1)	(2.4)	(2.4)
After caring	28	18	14
	(2.9)	(2.0)	(1.6)
Mean % of adult life in part-time work			
Prior to caring	15	14	10
	(1.6)	(1.3)	(9.8)
During caring	25	30	19
	(3.1)	(2.6)	(2.1)
After caring	33	27	14
	(3.1)	(2.3)	(1.7)
N	180	237	266

Source: Retirement Survey, Great Britain, 1988

which had elapsed since caring ceased had been spent in paid work, in comparison with the periods before and during caring (Table 34). Here we can see a distinctly lower average proportion of time spent in full-time work while caring lasts compared with prior to caring. In general this proportion falls further once caring stops. Prior to caring men had spent close to 100%[9] of their adult lives in full-time employment on average. During caring, men in the cohort aged 55–59 at the time of the survey spent on average 86% of the time they were caring in full-time work, those aged 60–64 spent 83% and those aged 65–69 only 79%. After caring ceased these proportions dropped still further. For women there were similar substantial falls in the proportion of time spent in full-time work during caring, but the proportion of time spent in part time work increased during caring, and for those in the youngest cohort increased still further once caring ceased. (The proportions spent in part-time work for men were extremely small.)

Clearly the patterns observed will be influenced by factors other than caring, many of which may be age related and therefore correlated with the passage of time. In particular the age at which caring stopped in relation to current age is important. By definition, past carers in the younger age groups will tend to have ceased caring at younger ages than those in the older age groups which will have had some effect on their subsequent employment histories. In order to investigate the effect of caring on subsequent employment it is therefore necessary to go beyond simple descriptive analyses of the type presented so far.

Investigating the effect of the length of time spent caring on subsequent employment

Cross-sectional analyses of the effect of caring on employment have provided evidence that those who devote many hours a week to caring are least likely to participate in paid work. Unfortunately, we are not able to tell from the Retirement Survey how many hours a week past carers spent caring. However, one might suspect that the longer caring lasts, the more detrimental it would be to subsequent employment opportunities. On the other hand, as we have already noted, long years spent caring may increase the financial imperative to take on paid work once caring ceases. In this section, we present the results of regression analysis which enables us to comment on the likelihood that a past carer will work at all after caring ceases, and how much of the time after caring ceases will be spent in work, depending on various factors including the length of time spent caring. The dependent variable in this analysis is the total amount of time, measured in years (and fractions of years[10]), since caring ceased, spent in paid work. Part-time work is counted as

---

[9] We have measured adult life from age 16 but some of the sample members first worked before that, so percentages can exceed 100.

[10] Work history spells are measured to the nearest whole month.

equivalent to one half of full time work. Since the dependent variable cannot be negative and is clustered at zero (considerable numbers of past carers did not work at all after ceasing to care), ordinary least squares regression is inappropriate. Instead, a 'Tobit' model was estimated in which the dependent variable was constrained to be not less than zero and not more than the time which had elapsed between ceasing to be a carer and the date interviewed in the Retirement Survey. This yields two estimated relationships. The first is the probability that a past carer will have worked at all since ceasing to care, and a set of explanatory variables. The second is between the total length of time spent in work since caring ceased, and those same explanatory variables. Explanatory variables covered obvious constraints on the dependent variables such as the length of time which had elapsed since caring ceased, dummy variables capturing socio-demographic characteristics and, of primary interest, the length of time spent caring. Where an explanatory variable might change over time perhaps as a result of caring, its value immediately before caring started was used. For example, social class (which is based on occupational characteristics which may change as a result of caring) is measured at that point. Separate models were estimated for men and women. The estimated coefficients are shown in Table 35.

The coefficients of a Tobit model are not directly interpretable: the effect of changes in one explanatory variable depends on the values of others. However one fact stands out. The coefficient on years cared is positive. Thus the longer someone has spent caring, the more likely they are to have worked since caring ceased and the longer they are likely to have spent in work, *other things being equal.* This could be interpreted as a financial effect or, perhaps as past carers wishing to work for the social and other non-financial benefits of working. Most other coefficients have the expected signs. Being in paid work when caring started increases the length of time in work after caring ceases, as does being in a skilled manual or higher social class. For women, having a child under the age of 5 when caring ceases reduces the length of time in work thereafter, controlling of course for factors such as the time which has elapsed since then.

It is important to stress that it is not the probability that a past carer will ever work again, nor the length of time he or she will ever work after caring ceases that is being estimated. It is the probability of working, and the length of time spent working, between ceasing to care and the date of being interviewed for the Retirement Survey. Thus we must always consider how long it has been since caring ceased in interpreting the estimates. For example, a man with average characteristics which imply about 7½ years caring ending when he was 53 and who is now 63 is predicted to have a 98% probability of working after caring ceases and to work for a total of just over 8 years out of the 10 available. If he were to have cared for 1 year more, the predicted

Table 35: Tobit estimates of years worked after caring ceased; by gender

Explanatory variable	Men			Women		
	Coefficient	Standard error	Mean of explan. var.	Coefficient	Standard error	Mean of explan. var.
Constant	23.960	4.890	1.000	24.301	4.259	1.000
Years cared	0.117	0.128	7.521	0.072	0.042	8.008
Age stopped caring	-1.108	0.124	52.655	-0.735	0.043	51.322
Years worked prior to caring	0.345	0.188	29.228	0.754	0.118	15.992
Square of above	-0.004	0.002	954.080	-0.015	0.003	346.700
Professional/managerial	1.115	0.815	0.271	0.614	0.856	0.146
Intermediate/skilled manual	0.876	0.669	0.552	0.265	0.571	0.451
In full-time work when caring started	3.268	1.327	0.925	4.171	0.711	0.341
In part-time work when caring started	0.808	2.675	0.008	3.278	0.701	0.258
Current age	0.501	0.063	62.580	0.088	0.066	62.668
Age fte ceased 18+	0.753	1.197	0.061	1.575	1.038	0.081
Aged > SPA when caring stopped	-2.420	1.778	0.052			
Single when caring stopped	-0.976	0.727	0.141	0.407	0.963	0.089
Widowed when caring stopped	-0.862	2.339	0.014	-0.818	1.338	0.050
Div/sep when caring stopped	-1.589	1.484	0.028			
Had child aged < 5 when caring stopped				-2.709	1.206	0.051
sigma	4.054	0.230		5.890	0.222	
Evaluated at mean values of explanatory variables:		std. err.			std. err.	
Probability years worked > 0	0.977	0.007		0.634	0.020	
Expected number of years worked	8.154	0.244		3.494	0.171	

increase in time in employment thereafter would be about 1½ months. The average female past carer had cared for 8 years, is also 63 and ceased caring 11 years ago. She is predicted to have a probability of having worked since caring ceased of 63% and a predicted time in work of 3½ years. If caring had lasted 1 year longer, the expect time in work would increase by 2½ weeks. Thus although we estimate a positive effect of the length of time spent caring on subsequent employment, it is small – at least for the average past carer.

Calculations based on the average person are useful for gauging the orders of magnitude of the estimated effects but they are somewhat unrealistic: the average man, for example, is part one social class and part another. A more satisfactory way to interpret the estimated model is to evaluate it at an initial set of characteristics and then again at perturbations from this. This is what is done in Table 36. The initial situation is based on median or modal values of the explanatory variables. For men this corresponds to someone who left school at age 14 and worked for a total of 30 years before caring started. At that point he was a skilled manual worker and was aged 49. He continued caring for 5 years, stopping at age 54. He was married at that point and is now aged 63. Our model gives him a 98% chance of working at some point after caring ceased and predicts he will have worked for a total of 8 years out of the 11 years which have elapsed. For women the base case is someone who left school at 14, accumulated a total of 13.75 years of paid work and was in a semi-skilled manual job before starting to care at age 48. She continued to care for 5 years, stopping at the age of 53. She was still married when she stopped caring and had no children under the age of 5. She is also 63 now so it has been 10 years since caring ceased. She is estimated to have had a 71% chance of working at some point after ceasing to care and expected to work for a total of nearly 4½ years.

There are many interesting variations from this base case that could be examined. We concentrate on the effect of shorter and longer periods spent caring and related variations in other explanatory variables. Such variations tend to have small effects for men. The exception to this is a variant in which although caring last for the same length of time as in the base case it starts 6 years later and so the man is aged 60 when caring stops. His chance of working at all in the time which has elapsed since ceasing to care is only 66%. However, at 2½ years, the expected length of time in work is high relative to the available time.

Variations from the base case have more effect for women. A woman caring for ten years rather than five, starting five years earlier, is predicted to have a chance of having worked after caring, of 60% compared with 70% for the base case; and an expected total time in paid work since caring ceased of three years rather than four. Thus the combined effect of caring for longer years

Table 36: Estimated effects of caring on post-caring employment; by gender

	Predicted probability of working at all after caring ceases (standard error)	Predicted total number of years worked after caring ceases (standard error)
	Men	
Base case	0.970 (.012)	7.650 (.598)
Variation from the base case:		
Cared for 10 years, starting 5 years earlier, worked for 25 years beforehand	0.967 (.013)	7.480 (.585)
Cared for 2 years, starting 2 years later, worked for 33 years beforehand	0.970 (.012)	7.670 (.624)
Started caring at age 55 having worked for 36 years and stopped at age 60	0.656 (.059)	2.563 (.444)
	Women	
Base case	0.708 (.044)	4.307 (.523)
Variation from base case:		
Cared for 10 years, starting 5 years earlier, worked for 8.75 years beforehand	0.600 (.052)	3.169 (.464)
Cared for 2 years, starting 3 years later, worked for 16.75 years beforehand	0.747 (.043)	4.806 (.562)
Worked for 5 years before caring and is now aged 69	0.451 (.099)	2.004 (.659)

Source: Retirement Survey, Great Britain, 1988

and starting earlier in life is to reduce the probability of working after caring stops and reduce the expected time spent in work, even though the amount of time available to work after caring stops is the same. Starting to care later in life for a shorter period increases employment prospects. A woman who cares for two years starting at age 51 having worked for nearly 17 years before caring is predicted to work for four years in the ten years since ceasing to care. On the other hand, belonging to an earlier generation (aged 69 now) with just five years work experience prior to caring reduces the probability of having worked since caring ceased to 45% with an expected total amount of time worked since then of just two years, even though more time has elapsed since caring ceased.

PENSION HISTORIES

We have seen that once age and gender differences are taken into account, there was not a great deal of difference between past carers and non-carers in the average proportions of adult life they had spent in paid employment. There were, however, some differences when the periods before, during and after caring were compared. In this section we draw similar comparisons for the proportions of time spent as members of occupational pension schemes. Table 37 is similar to Table 32 but shows the mean proportions of adult life spent as a member of an occupational pension scheme. Periods belonging to schemes where the pension rights were cashed-in or lost are not counted.

Differences in occupational pension coverage between past carers and non-carers were small. Only amongst men aged 65–69 was the average proportion

Table 37: Proportion of adult life spent in pensionable employment; by age and gender

	Men aged:		
	55–59	60–64	65–69
Mean % of adult life in pensionable employment			
Past-carers	34	35	29
	(3.0)	(2.6)	(2.2)
N	114	125	143
Non-carers	31	35	33
	(1.7)	(1.6)	(1.6)
N	356	347	286
	Women aged:		
	55–59	60–64	65–69
Mean % of adult life spent in pensionable employment			
Past-carers	14	10	9
	(1.6)	(1.2)	(1.1)
N	193	247	281
Non-carers	14	8	6
	(1.5)	(0.9)	(0.9)
N	231	263	204

Source: Retirement Survey, Great Britain, 1988

of adult life spent as a member of an occupational pension scheme smaller than that for non-carers. Amongst women, past carers had spent higher proportions of their adult lives in a pension scheme members than non-carers except in the youngest age groups where the mean proportions were the same. The differences in coverage rates of the proportions for men and women – whether past carers or not – are, of course, very marked, however.

Those who had cared for more than ten years had generally spent lower proportions of their adult lives in pensionable employment than those who had cared for shorter periods (Table 38). The only exception to this was in the oldest age group, but here the difference is not statistically significant. Amongst men in the youngest cohort, the mean proportion of adult life spent in pensionable employment of those who had cared for at least ten years was not much more than half that of those who had cared for less than ten years. Similarly for women in the two youngest age groups who had cared for at least ten years, the proportions of life spent in pensionable employment were only half those of women who had cared for shorter periods.

Table 38: Proportion of adult life spent in pensionable employment; by age and gender and whether people had cared for fewer or more than ten years

	Men aged:		
	55–59	60–64	65–69
Mean % of adult life in pensionable employment			
<10 years	39	38	27
	(3.6)	(3.0)	(2.7)
N	82	88	101
>10 years	21	28	34
	(4.5)	(4.7)	(4.1)
N	32	37	42
	Women aged:		
	55–59	60–64	65–69
Mean % of adult life spent in pensionable employment			
<10 years	17	12	8
	(2.0)	(1.6)	(1.2)
N	143	171	183
>10 years	8	6	10
	(2.4)	(1.7)	(2.1)
N	50	76	98

Source: Retirement Survey, Great Britain, 1988

Looking at the periods before, during and after caring, we see a quite different pattern from that for employment patterns: pension coverage rates are higher during caring than prior to caring. For the youngest age cohort they increase still further after caring ceases (Table 39). This is most likely to reflect the general growth over time in occupational pension coverage but it is remarkable that this outweighs the downward movement in participation in full-time work which we have seen occurred as past carers pass though their period of caring.

Table 39: Proportion of adult life spent in pensionable employment, during and after caring; by age and gender

	Men aged:		
	55–59	60–64	65–69
Mean % of adult life in pensionable employment			
Prior to caring	25	27	22
	(3.1)	(2.8)	(2.3)
During caring	35	43	39
	(4.2)	(4.6)	(3.7)
After caring	39	40	25
	(4.2)	(3.7)	(2.7)
N	114	125	143
	Women aged:		
	55–59	60–64	65–69
Mean % of adult life in pensionable employment			
Prior to caring	8	7	6
	(1.5)	(1.1)	(1.1)
During Caring	17	15	11
	(2.7)	(2.0)	(1.8)
After caring	22	12	6
	(2.8)	(1.7)	(1.0)
N	193	247	281

Source: Retirement Survey, Great Britain, 1988

SUMMARY

In this chapter we have seen that men who were past carers were generally less likely to be in a job than non-carers. Under state pension age women who were past carers were slightly less likely to be in paid work than non-carers but beyond state pension age they were more likely to have a job.

Perhaps surprisingly, there were few differences between past carers and non-carers in the proportions of total adult life spent in employment. An exception was that amongst women aged 55–59 years and 60–64 years, the average proportion of adult life spent in full-time employment was lower for those who had spent more than ten years caring than for women who had cared for shorter periods.

There is evidence from our analysis of the length of time that past carers spent in employment after caring ceased, that they attempted to make up for lost time. The longer they had spent caring, the longer they seemed to spend in work after caring ceased (controlling for other relevant factors including the length of time available to them). However, what is also important, is how early in life caring started. Someone starting to care in later life is likely to work for longer after caring ceases than someone caring for a similar length of time but starting earlier in life. These effects seem to be stronger for women than for men.

As elsewhere, the strongest finding on pension histories is that caring for long periods of time was associated with markedly lower accumulation of pension rights than caring for shorter periods. This was especially true for women where those in the age groups 55–59 and 60–64 who had cared for more than ten years had, on average, contributed to an occupational pension for only half as many years as those caring for shorter periods.

5 MARRIAGE, CHILD-BEARING AND HOME MOVES

Caring may affect family formation and dissolution. Although Parker and Lawton (1994) found little evidence that caring altered chances of marrying, they did find that the most heavily involved carers were the most likely to be single. In this section we present some analysis of past carers' marital states when they ceased caring and at the point at which they were subsequently interviewed in the Retirement Survey. For women, we also look at how many children they had had at these same points. A brief analysis of home moves after caring is also presented.

MARRIAGE

Table 40 shows the marital states of past carers at the end of the year in which caring ceased. Over 80% of past carers were married (or cohabiting) at this point. Five per cent of women but only 1% of men were widowed. Obviously this may have been related to the cessation of caring if the cared-for person was a spouse whose death had been the reason why caring stopped. Quite high proportions of past carers – particularly past male carers – had never been married at the time caring ceased. The proportions were highest amongst those who were under 40 when their caring ceased: 26% for men and 16% for women. However, even amongst those whose caring stopped at later ages the proportions who had never been married were quite high, especially amongst men. Some 14% of men who stopped caring when they were aged 40 or more had never been married.

Table 40: Marital status of past carers when caring ceased;, by gender and age when caring ceased

	Men (%)					
Age when caring stopped	married	single	widowed	divorced/ separated	Total	N
Under 40	74	26	–		100	32
40–49	83	14	2	1	100	83
50–59	81	14	1	5	100	177
60+	81	13	2	4	100	90
All	81	15	1	4	100	382
	Women (%)					
Age when caring stopped	married	single	widowed	divorced/ separated	Total	N
Under 40	85	16	–	–	100	99
40–49	85	10	1	4	100	140
50–59	83	9	5	3	100	332
60+	80	6	11	4	100	150
All	83	9	5	3	100	721

Source: Retirement Survey, Great Britain, 1988

Table 41: Changes in marital status since caring ceased; by gender and age when caring ceased

Men (%)

Age when caring stopped	no change in marital status				change in marital status			Total
	married	single	widowed	div/sep	single to married	married to widowed	married to div/sep	
Under 40	63	9	–	–	17	9	3	100
40–49	69	12	2	1	1	9	5	100
50–59	76	13	1	4	½	4	1	100
60+	63	13	2	4	–	17	1	100
All	70	13	1	3	2	8	2	100

Women (%)

Age when caring stopped	no change in marital status				change in marital status			Total
	married	single	widowed	divorced/separated	single to married	married to widowed	married to div/sep	
Under 40	58	5	–	–	9	20	6	100
40–49	63	9	1	3	1	21	1	100
50–59	61	9	5	3	–	19	2	100
60+	46	6	10	4	–	32	1	100
All	58	8	5	3	1	23	2	100

Source: Retirement Survey, Great Britain, 1988
Note: Percentages sum to less than 100 because other changes in marital states occurred in small numbers.

Altogether, 87% of men and 74% of women had the same marital status at the time they were interviewed as when their caring stopped (Table 41). The most common change in marital status was from married to widowed. Eight per cent of men and 23% of women were widowed some time between when caring ceased and being interviewed for the Retirement Survey. Seventeen per cent of men who were aged under 40 when they stopped caring, and 9% of women, subsequently married for the first time.

In order to put these figures into perspective, some comparisons are shown in Tables 42 and 43 of past carers' and non-carers' marital histories. They show what proportions of past carers and non-carers had ever been married by selected ages, and of those who had, what percentages were widowed, divorced or separated by those ages. At each age shown, smaller proportions

Table 42: Proportion of past carers and non-carers ever married at selected ages; by gender

	Men			
	at age 40	at age 49	at age 59	N
Past carers	86	87	87	989
Non-carers	92	93	95	382
	Women			
	at age 40	at age 49	at age 59	N
Past carers	90	91	92	721
Non carers	95	96	96	698

Source: Retirement Survey, Great Britain, 1988

Table 43: Proportion of ever married past carers and non-carers who were widowed, separated or divorced at selected ages; by gender

	Men			
	at age 40	at age 49	at age 59	N
Past carers	2	6	9	989
Non-carers	4	6	9	382
	Women			
	at age 40	at age 49	at age 59	N
Past carers	5	10	23	721
Non carers	4	9	18	698

Source: Retirement Survey, Great Britain, 1988

of men and women past carers than non-carers had ever been married. For example, amongst non-carers 92% of men and 85% of women had been married by the age of 40. Amongst past carers, the corresponding proportions were 86% and 90%. By age 59, 9% of male past carers and 23% of female past carers who had ever been married, were widowed, divorced or separated. Amongst non-carers the comparative figures were 9% and 18%. The differences between past carers and non-carers were almost entirely accounted for by greater proportions of past carers being widowed by age 59. This may, of

Table 44: Current marital states, past carers and non carers; by age and gender

	Men aged:		
	55–59	60–64	65–69
Past carers			
married/cohabiting	72	78	68
never married	17	11	11
widowed	5	5	18
divorced/separated	6	6	3
N	114	125	143
Non-carers			
married/cohabiting	88	83	81
never married	3	6	7
widowed	2	3	7
divorced/separated	7	8	5
N	356	347	286
	Women aged:		
	55–59	60–64	65–69
Past carers			
married/cohabiting	74	56	52
never married	7	8	9
widowed	12	32	35
divorced/separated	8	4	4
N	193	247	281
Non-carers			
married/cohabiting	83	75	60
never married	3	6	3
widowed	9	14	31
divorced/separated	5	5	6
N	231	263	204

Source: Retirement Survey, Great Britain, 1988

course, simply reflect the fact that past carers may have been looking after spouses who died relatively young.

Differences in marital histories between past carers and non-carers are reflected in their current marital states (Table 44). In all age cohorts, past carers were more likely to be never married than non-carers but the difference was particularly marked for those aged 55–59. Seventeen per cent of male past carers aged 55–59 at the time of the Retirement Survey had never been married compared with only 3% of men of the same age who had never been a carer. The corresponding figures for women are 7% and 3%.

CHILD-BEARING

Ninety-seven per cent of women had had at least one child by the time they ceased caring, over a third had had three or more children (Table 45). By the time of the Retirement Survey, 9% had had at least one additional child. Fourteen percent of those whose caring stopped when they were under 40 had their first child subsequently.

As with marital histories, some comparisons between past carers and non-carers are needed to help us to interpret these findings. Table 46 shows the proportions of women who had born a child by age 40, by age cohort. In the

Table 45: Fertility amongst women past carers; by age when caring ceased

Proportions bearing the following number of children by the time caring ceased:					
Age when caring stopped	0	1	2	3+	Total
Under 40	14	25	30	31	100
40–49	1	29	42	29	100
50–59	1	22	37	39	100
60+	0	24	43	33	100
All	3	24	38	35	100
Proportions bearing the following number of children subsequently:					
Age when caring stopped	0	1	2	3+	Total
Under 40	47	20	22	11	100
40–49	98	1	1	1	100
50–59	99	1	0	0	100
60+	100	0	0	0	100
All	91	4	3	2	100

Source: Retirement Survey, Great Britain, 1988

Table 46: Proportions of women who had borne a child by age 40, past carers and non-carers; by current age

	Current age:		
	55–59	60–64	65–69
Past carers			
0 children (%)	13	21	20
1 child (%)	17	17	21
2 children (%)	32	33	33
3+ children (%)	38	30	27
N	193	247	281
Non-carers			
0 children (%)	15	18	15
1 child (%)	15	19	24
2 children (%)	30	32	37
3+ children (%)	41	32	25
N	231	263	204

Source: *Retirement Survey, Great Britain, 1988*

two oldest age cohorts (those currently aged 60–64 and 65–69), the proportions who had not had a child by age 40 were lower amongst past carers than non-carers. A fifth of past carers in these cohorts had not had a child by age 40, compared with 18% of non-carers currently aged 60–64 and 15% of non-carers aged 65–69. Other than amongst the oldest cohort, past carers were less likely than non-carers to have had three or more children by the time they had reached 40. However, the differences between past carers and non-carers are all quite small and generally not as great as the differences between cohorts. The youngest cohort was substantially more likely to have had three or more children by age 40 than the two older cohorts.

HOME MOVES

A quarter of men and a third of women had moved house since they ceased to care. Those whose caring stopped at younger ages were more likely to have moved than those who were older when caring ceased. Women who ceased caring in their sixties were markedly more likely to have moved than their male counterparts. Fifteen per cent of women who ceased caring aged 60 or more had since moved compared with 6% of men.

People who had moved since 1974 were asked what factors affected their decisions to move. More than eighty per cent of past carers who had moved since ceasing to care had done so since 1974. These include all those who were aged 50 or more when they ceased to care and more than 70% of those who ceased to care at younger ages. The most common reasons for moving are shown in Table 47 for both past carers and non-carers who had moved since 1974. Respondents were permitted to give more than one reason.

Amongst past carers, the largest proportions of both men and women said that they moved to live in a more convenient or manageable house: 44% and 51% respectively. Twenty-three per cent of men and 17% of women moved to be nearer friends/relatives. Thirteen per cent gave their own ill-health as a reason for moving. Women were more likely than men to give their spouse's ill-health as a reason for moving – 7% compared with only 1%, and to move as a result of the death of their spouse: 10% compared with 1%. Men were slightly more likely to move as a result of the death of a relative other than spouse or of a friend – 5% compared with 3% for women. Fourteen per cent of men and 11 per cent of women moved to save or make money. Actual or approaching retirement was also a common reason.

Comparing male past carers and non-carers, the latter were less likely to move in order to live in a more convenient or manageable house, or to be nearer friends or relatives. Non-carers were more likely to move in order to live in a better area and as a result of approaching or actual retirement. Amongst women the main differences between past carers and non-carers was that non-carers were far less likely to give 'living in a more convenient/manageable house' as a reason for moving and slightly more likely to move 'to be nearer

Table 47: Reasons for moving house, past carers and non-carers who had moved since ceasing to care and since 1974; by gender

	Men		Women	
	past carers	non-carers	past carers	non-carers
To live in a more convenient/manageable house (%)	44	35	51	32
To live in a better area (%)	25	30	27	23
To be nearer friends/relatives (%)	23	13	17	21
To live in the country/by the sea (%)	15	11	8	10
To be nearer shops/services (%)	11	8	10	8
Own ill health (%)	13	9	13	9
Spouse's ill-health (%)	1	2	7	1
Death of spouse (%)	1	1	10	6
Death of other relative/friend (%)	5	2	3	1
To save/make money (%)	14	11	11	11
Approaching/actual retirement (%)	12	17	17	17
N	76	426	183	311

Source: Retirement Survey, Great Britain, 1988

friends or relatives'. Non-carers were less likely to have moved because of their own ill-health, or in the case of women, the ill-health or death of their spouse.

SUMMARY

The analysis in this chapter has revealed some interesting differences in the paths that past carers and non-carers lives have taken. Past carers, especially men, were less likely to be or have been married by the time they reached the age of forty, than non-carers. In all age groups covered by the Retirement Survey, past carers were more likely to be never-married than non-carers but the difference was particularly marked for those past carers currently aged 55–59. Seventeen per cent of male past carers aged 55–59 had never been married compared with 3% of men of the same age who had not been a carer.

More women than men were widows when their caring ceased. Few men or women who ceased caring after the age of forty subsequently married for the first time. However, men who ceased to care under the age of forty were more likely to marry subsequently for the first time than women.

Only in the oldest of the three cohorts (that is those aged 65–69) were female past carers more likely to have been childless at the age of forty. More than one half of women who ceased caring under the age of forty subsequently had at least one more child.

A quarter of men and a third of women had moved house since they ceased to care. Of those who had moved house since 1974, the reason given most often by past carers and non-carers, men and women alike, was in order to move to a more convenient or manageable house. Past carers were more likely than non-carers to give their ill-health, or in the case of women, their spouse's ill-health or death, as a reason for moving.

6 SUMMARY AND CONCLUSIONS

The vital role of carers is now beyond question. Their contribution is lauded by politicians: carers may be seen as reducing the drain on the public purse, but also as fulfilling a role which is usually what they and the cared-for person want. Over the last decade or so our knowledge of the extent of informal caring, and what it means for those involved, has grown enormously. We have learnt of the problems – and rewards – of care-giving, from in-depth small scale-scale research. In 1988, national estimates of the numbers of carers and analyses of who provides most of this care, were published for the first time. These were made possible by the inclusion of relevant questions in the 1985 General Household Survey (GHS) and have recently been updated, based on the 1990 GHS.

Previous research has concentrated on the experiences of people while they are providing care. The possibility that caring continues to have consequences even after it has ceased has also emerged as a matter for concern, but until now has not been researched at the national level. Few studies have been able to look back at a period when a person was a carer to see what effect that had subsequently on their lives. At a national level, the data have not existed.

Over 1,000 people who had cared for someone in the past are the subject of this study. They come from a nationally representative survey – the Retirement Survey – of 3,500 people aged 55–69 and their partners outside this age range. The Retirement Survey provides a rare opportunity to study people's experiences before, during and after caring. Although not designed specifically with this in mind, the survey included a number of questions which asked about caring in the past and its effects. The survey also collected information on people's working lives. It has thus been possible to study the relationship between periods spent caring and periods spent working full or part-time for the first time.

A strength of the Retirement Survey is that it contains some evidence on past carers' own views of the effects caring had had on their lives. However, we must acknowledge, in common with existing research on current carers, that where differences between past carers and non-carers have been found they may not be the *effect* of caring. Instead they may reflect differences between people who *become* carers and those who do not.

In this Chapter we bring together and summarise our findings. We highlight some common threads which run through the topics we have covered and review the main findings from each Chapter, drawing attention to some policy issues which arise. Our findings also point to areas where further research is needed.

SOME COMMON THREADS

There are four common threads which run through our findings. The first is in keeping with existing research on current carers. Differences between past carers *en masse* and non-carers are small, once relevant factors such as gender are taken into account. Thus generalisations are unhelpful and may mislead. Policies aimed at helping carers and encouraging their supply, run the risk of being seen as expensive and ineffectual if they do not take this finding on board.

If generalisations are not valid, then what are the important characteristics which influence the long term effects of caring? Research on current carers has shown the importance of distinguishing between those for whom caring takes up many hours a week and those who provide lower levels of care. The corresponding finding from our analysis – our second common thread – is the distinction between carers who have devoted many years to caring and those for whom caring lasted for shorter periods. Once past carers were divided into those who had cared for fewer than and more than ten years, consistent differences emerged. Longer-term past carers had lower incomes, were more likely to be in receipt of means-tested benefits, and had spent less time as members of occupational pensions than those who had cared for shorter periods. We cannot say from our data whether the long hours and long years go hand-in-hand. Nor do we know the kind of care provided – another factor known to be important in distinguishing current carers. However, it is clearly important that the length of time someone has spent, or is likely to spend, being a carer is taken into account in policy formation.

The third common thread is that differences between the incomes, employ-ment and pension records of men on the one hand, and women on the other, dwarf any differences between past carers and non-carers, even when the length of time spent caring is taken into account.

Following on from this is our fourth and final common thread. Again, in line with previous research on current carers, we find that, in general, differences between past carers and non-carers are greater for women than men. We must stress, as others have done, that this probably says more about the factors which effect whether someone *becomes* a carer than about the *effects* of caring itself. It may be that men become carers only if they can combine caring with a normal or near-normal career.

The policy issues which arise from the third and fourth common thread are relevant not just to carers. They are of general relevance to any policy which seeks to make it easier for women – and men – to combine work and family life.

SELF-REPORTED EFFECTS OF CARING

For some past carers, but not the majority, caring was perceived as having had a detrimental effect on their working lives. The self-reported effects of caring on various aspects of past carers' employment and earnings were relatively small. Only 7% of men and 9% of women said that caring had had an effect on their retirement plans. Fourteen per cent of men – but over a quarter of women – either lost a job, took a lower paid job, had difficulty getting a job, or lost pay because of their caring responsibilities. The large majority of both men and women reported no effect at all of caring on their employment or retirement plans.

THE CURRENT INCOMES OF PAST CARERS

Caring has long term financial consequences which affect carers after caring has ceased. The differences that we have found between the incomes of past carers and non-carers are, for the most part, consistent with analyses of current carers in the General Household Survey. Male carers in the GHS, for example, have lower incomes than male non-carers, but the average weekly income of female carers was little different from that of non-carers. We found from the Retirement Survey that male past carers have mean weekly incomes of £13 (retired) and £17 (non-retired) less than non-carers, but that female past carers actually had higher weekly incomes than non-carers. Male past carers generally live in families that have slightly lower incomes than those of non-carers, although the difference is small and the margin of error relatively large. The family incomes of female retired past carers are slightly higher than those of non-carers, although the differences are not statistically significant.

However, several points of interest have emerged from our analysis of the Retirement Survey. The clearest finding is that people who had cared for more than ten years were financially disadvantaged in almost all respects compared with both non-carers and with people who had cared for shorter periods. This is true of both retired and non-retired people, and of both men and women. The differentials are relatively large: retired men who had cared for more than ten years had mean weekly incomes of £7 lower than retired men who had cared for fewer than ten years. The mean income gap for retired women was £11. For non-retired men the mean income gap was £21, and for non-retired women the mean income gap was £28. Although for men the differences are subject to side margins of error, we can be highly confident that women past carers have significantly lower incomes than non-carers. Non-retired women who had cared for more than ten years have mean incomes of around three-fifths that of similar women who had cared for fewer than ten years or who had not cared at all.

Figure 4: Mean weekly income (£s) by gender, carer and retirement status

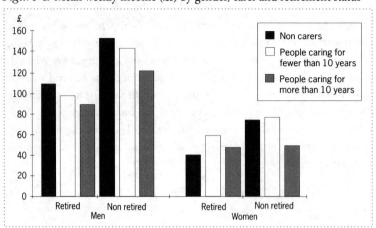

The family incomes of people who had cared for more than ten years were considerably lower than those of people who had cared for fewer than ten years. Non-retired men who had cared for more than ten years had family incomes of £16 a week lower than those whose period of caring was shorter. For non-retired women the differences were proportionally greater: they tend to live in families with incomes of only four-fifths those of women who had cared for fewer than ten years.

Differences are not as substantial, but are still clear, when we compare people who reported that caring had had an adverse effect on their working lives with people who did not report an effect. Sample sizes for men are very small, but non-retired women who reported an adverse effect on working life had mean incomes of £15 a week lower than women who reported no effect. Families in which a man or woman was a past carer who had reported that caring had had an effect on their working lives had incomes lower than those families where the past carer reported no effect. This is especially true of non-retired women who live in families with incomes around three-quarters that of non-retired women who reported no effect.

Gender differentials in income, however, dwarf the differences between sub-groups of carers. Retired male non-carers, for example, have mean weekly personal incomes two and a half times higher than those of retired female non-carers. Non-retired male non-carers have weekly incomes more than twice the average for non-retired female non-carers. Even the worst-off group of male past carers (retired men who had cared for more than ten years) had mean weekly incomes of £14 higher than the best-off groups of women identified (non-retired women who had cared for fewer than ten years). Gender differentials persist through all the components of income that we examined: male non-carers earn on average more than twice as much from employment when working, seven times as much from occupational and private pensions when retired, and six times as much from state benefits when retired (excluding the retirement pension) than women.

Past caring, however, clearly has real and substantial effects on income, and this is reflected in many of the components of total income. Past carers still in employment at the time of the survey, for example, had considerably lower incomes from employment compared with non-carers. Men who had cared for fewer than ten years earned £8 a week on average more than men who had cared for more than ten years; for women the figure was £22 a week – two-thirds of the income from employment of women who had cared for fewer than ten years.

Families of past carers are more likely to depend on means-tested benefits to get by than families of non-carers. Almost twice the proportion of retired men who reported that caring had had an effect on their working lives received means-tested benefits, compared with non-carers. For both men and women, past carers who reported an effect of caring on their working lives were significantly more likely to be in receipt of means-tested benefits than past carers who reported no effect.

Figure 5: Proportions of retired people receiving means tested benefits, by gender and carer status

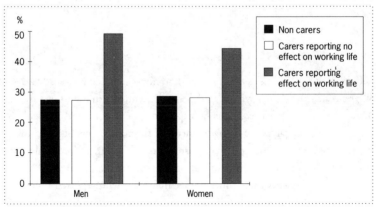

Some surprising and unexpected findings have also emerged from our analysis of the Retirement Survey. Analysis of the General Household Survey found that current carers who provided the most intensive levels of care had substantially lower incomes from savings than non-carers. Here, however, we find that past carers are *more* likely to have savings, and have higher incomes from saving, than non-carers. People who had cared for fewer than ten years tended to have the highest incomes from savings of all: retired men earned £7 a week more from investment income than non-carers, whilst non-retired women earned £5 a week more.

Figure 6: Mean weekly income from savings of retired people, by gender and carer status

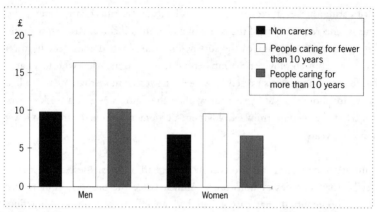

We cannot be sure why this is. Inheritance may play a part, but the policy implications are likely to be controversial. The current capital rules for Income Support and Housing Benefit exclude from benefit, or reduce the benefit entitlement of, people who have relatively large amounts of capital even if their total income is low. Our analysis suggests that past carers may be one of the groups who fall into this trap.

EMPLOYMENT AND PENSION HISTORIES

Differences in the incomes of past carers and non-carers can be traced back to differences in their employment and pension records, although these differences were not as great as might be expected. Non-carers, and particularly male retired non-carers, have *higher* incomes from state benefits (excluding the state retirement pension) than past carers. However, retired male past carers who reported an effect of caring on their working life had mean incomes from benefits three times higher than men who reported no effect.

Men aged 55–59 years and men aged 65–69 years who were past carers were generally less likely to be in a job than non-carers. In the older of these two age groups, that is those within their first five years of reaching state pension age, only 6% of past carers had a job, compared with 13% of non-carers. Beyond state pension age, women past carers were *more* likely to be in paid work than non-carers. However, past carers generally worked fewer hours per week than non-carers; and women were much more likely to work part-time than men.

There were surprisingly small differences in the proportions of their lives that past carers and non-carers spent in paid work. However, except in the oldest age group (those aged 65–69), amongst women past carers, the average proportion of adult life spent in full-time work was noticeably lower for those who had been carers for more than ten years compared with those who had cared for fewer than ten years (38% compared with 44% in the age group 55–59 years; 35% compared with 43% in the age group 60–64). Differences in the proportions for men and women were again much more stark than between carers and non-carers (Figure 7).

Figure 7: Proportions of adult life spent in full time work, non carers, people caring for fewer or more than 10 years

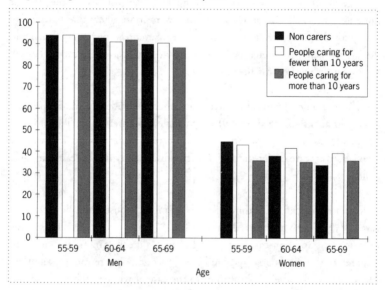

Our analysis of the length of time past carers spent in paid work after their caring responsibilities ended, suggests that they may attempt to make up for lost time. Controlling for other relevant factors, the longer a carer had spent caring, the longer he or she spent in paid work thereafter. However, starting to care earlier in life seemed to be detrimental to employment prospects once caring ceased; and the apparent effect was stronger for women than men. In terms of social security policy there are thus some direct parallels with the effects of disability. Changes to benefits for disabled people introduced in recent years were designed to recognise the effects that early on-set of disability had on a disabled person's prospects of earning a living. Our analysis suggests that similar considerations ought to play a part in the development of employment and benefits policies for carers.

OTHER IMPORTANT LIFE EVENTS

There were some clear differences between the family formation patterns of past carers and non-carers although this may not have been an effect of caring. Past carers, especially men, were less likely to be or have been married by the time they reached the age of forty, than non-carers. Fourteen per cent of male past carers were unmarried at the age of forty, compared with only 8% of non-carers. For women the equivalent proportions were 10% and 5%.

In each age group covered by the Retirement Survey, past carers were more likely to be never-married than non-carers but the differences were particularly marked for those aged 55–59. Seventeen per cent of male past carers in this age group were never-married compared with just 3% of men of the same age who had not been carers. Men were more likely than women to marry for the first time after ceasing to care. Seventeen per cent of men and 9% of women who were aged under 40 at the time their caring ceased, subsequently married for the first time.

Only in the oldest of the three five-year cohorts included in the Retirement Survey (that is those aged 65–69) were female past carers more likely to have been childless at the age of forty than non-carers. More than 50% of women who ceased to care under the age of forty subsequently had at least one more child.

A quarter of women and a third of men had moved house since they ceased to care. Of those who had moved house since 1974, the reason given most often by past carers and non-carers, men and women alike, was in order to move to a more convenient or manageable house. Past carers were more likely than non-carers to give their ill-health, or in the case of women, their spouse's ill-health or death, as a reason for moving.

AREAS FOR FURTHER RESEARCH

A number of our findings are difficult to explain, for example that past carers had higher incomes from savings than non-carers. One can hypothesise that this was due to inheritances, perhaps from the person for whom they were caring but we cannot know if this is the case without new research.

Some of our findings beg questions which cannot be answered from the Retirement Survey. Although the importance of the number of years a carer spent caring is very clear, we cannot say, for example, whether those who care for long periods also devote many hours a week to caring. Nor have we been able to distinguish between those who cared for someone with whom they lived and those caring for someone living elsewhere; or to distinguish those caring for a child, from those caring for a spouse or parent.

Perhaps more importantly we do not know why caring ended. The financial consequences (to say nothing of the emotional effects), for example, of the death of a cared-for person will be very different from those which follow a cared-for person entering residential care.

Finally, our analysis has been restricted to a particular age group and a particular generation. The effects of past caring may be different at other ages and for other generations may be different.

Our research has thus emphasised the need to consider the long term effects in policy areas which span social security, housing, pensions and employment, policies specifically for carers and family policies in general. When carers cease to be "carers" they are not transformed overnight into "non-carers".

REFERENCES

Arber, S and Ginn, J (1990) The meaning of informal care: gender and the contribution of elderly people *Ageing and Society*, 10, 4: 429–454

Arber, S and Ginn, J (1991) *Gender and later life* Sage, London

Askham, J et al., (1992) *Caring: the importance of third age carers*, Carnegie Inquiry into the Third Age, Research Paper 6, Carnegie UK Trust, Dunfermline

Baldwin, S (1994) Love and money: the financial consequences of caring for an older relative, in Policy Studies Institute, *The future of family care for elderly people*, PSI, London (forthcoming)

Baldwin, SM and Parker, G (1994), Support for informal carers - the role of social security, in Dalley, G (ed.) *Disability and social policy*, Policy Studies Institute, London

Berthoud, R (1991) Meeting the costs of disability, in Dalley, G (ed) *Disability and social policy* Policy Studies Institute, London

Bone, M, Gregory, J, Gill, B and Loder, D (1992) *Retirement and retirement plans* HMSO, London

Charlesworth, A, Wilkin, D and Durie, A (1984) *Carers and services: a comparison of men and women caring for dependent elderly people* Equal Opportunities Commission, London

Department of Health (1991) *Carer support in the community: evaluation of the Department of Health initiative: 'demonstration districts for informal carers' 1986–1989* HMSO, London

Department of Social Security (1993) *Social Security Statistics 1993* HMSO, London

Evandrou, M (1987) *The use of domiciliary services by the elderly: a survey* London School of Economics: Welfare State Programme, 15

Evandrou, M (1991) Challenging invisibility of carers: mapping informal care nationally in Laczko, F and Victor, C (eds) *Social policy and elderly people: the role of community care* Avebury, Aldershot

Evandrou, M, Arber, S, Dale, A and Gilbert, N (1986) Who cares for the elderly? Family care provision and receipt of statutory services, in Phillipson, C, Bernard, M and Strang, P (eds) *Dependency and interdependency in old age - theoretical perspectives and policy alternatives* Croom Helm, London

Evandrou, M and Winter, D (1989) *Informal carers and the labour market in Britain* Welfare State Programme, WSP/89 STICERD, LSE

Family Policy Studies Centre (1989) *Family Policy Bulletin 6* FPSC, London

Foster, K, Wilmot, A and Dobbs, J (1990) *General Household Survey 1988*, series GHS no. 19, HMSO, London

Glendinning, C (1988) Dependency and interdependency: the incomes of informal carers and the impact of social security in Baldwin, S, Parker, G and Walker, R (eds) *Social security and community care* Avebury, Aldershot

Glendinning, C (1989) *The financial circumstances of informal carers: final report* SPRU, York

Glendinning, C (1992) *The costs of informal care: looking inside the household* SPRU Discussion Paper, HMSO: London

Glendinning, C and McLaughlin, E (1993) Paying for informal care: lessons from Finland *Journal of European Social Policy*, 3 (4): 239–253

Green, H (1988) General Household Survey (GHS) *Informal carers* HMSO, London

Grundy, E (1992) Socio-demographic change, in Central Health Monitoring Unit *The Health of Elderly People, an Epidemiological Overview: Companion Papers*, HMSO: London

HM Treasury (1989) *The Government's expenditure plans 1989–90 to 1991–92* Cm 601–621 HMSO, London

Joshi, H (1987) The cost of caring, in Glendinning, C and Millar, J *Women and Poverty in Britain* Harvester Press, Brighton

Joshi, H (1994) The labour market and unpaid caring: conflict and compromise, in Policy Studies Institute, *The future of family care for elderly people*, PSI: London (forthcoming)

Laczko, F and Noden, S (1991) Eldercare and the labour market: combining care and work in Laczko, F and Victor, C (eds) *Social policy and elderly people: the role of community care* Avebury, Aldershot

Laczko, F and Noden, S (1992) Combining paid work with eldercare: the implications for social policy *Health and Social Care*, 1: 81–89

Laczko, F and Phillipson, C (1991) *Changing work and retirement: social policy and the older worker* Open University Press, Milton Keynes

Lewis, J and Meredith, B (1988) *Daughters who care: daughters caring for mothers at home* Routledge, London

Martin, J and White, A (1988) *The financial circumstances of disabled adults living in private households*, HMSO, London

Matthewman, J (1991) *Tolley's social security and state benefits, 1991–92* Tolley Publishing Company Ltd, Croydon

Matthews, A and Truscott, P (1990) *Disability, household income and expenditure: a follow-up survey of disabled adults in the Family Expenditure Survey*, DSS Research Report, no. 2, HMSO, London

McLaughlin, E (1991) *Social security and community care: the case of the invalid care allowance* HMSO, London

National Economic and Development Council (NEDO) (1989) *Defusing the demographic timebomb* HMSO, London

Nissel, M and Bonnerjea, L (1982) *Family care of the handicapped elderly: who pays?* Policy Studies Institute, London

OPCS (1992) General Household Survey: Carers in 1990 *OPCS Monitor, SS 92/2* HMSO, London

OPCS (1993) *Census: sex, age and marital status, Great Britain*, HMSO, London

Parker, G (1989) *The same difference? The experience of men and women caring for a spouse with a disability or chronic illness* DHSS 571 7/89 SPRU, York

Parker, G (1990) *With due care and attention: a review of the literature on informal care* Family Policy Studies Centre, London

Parker, G and Lawton, D (1992) *Further analysis of the GHS data on informal carers, Report 4: Male carers* Social Policy Research Unit, University of York, York

Parker, G and Lawton, D (1994) *Different types of care, different types of carer: evidence from the General Household Survey* SPRU, HMSO, London

Pudney, S and Sutherland, H (1992) "The Statistical Reliability of Micro-simulation Estimates: Results for a UK Tax-Benefit Model" in *Micro-simulation Models for Public Policy Analysis: New Frontiers*, Hancock, R and Sutherland, H (eds), STICERD Occasional Paper No. 17, STICERD, LSE, London.

Tinker, A, McCreadie, C and Hancock, R (1992) The financial costs of caring, in Askham, J, Grundy, E and Tinker, A *Caring: the importance of third age carers* Carnegie UK Trust, Dunfermline

Twigg, J and Atkin, K (1994) *Carers perceived: policy and practice in informal care* Open University Press, Buckingham

APPENDIX: DATA AND METHODS
OF ANALYSIS

THE RETIREMENT SURVEY, 1988

The source for our study was the Survey of Retirement and Retirement Plans of 1988, which was carried out by the Office of Population Censuses and Surveys. The sample consists of around 3,500 people aged 55–69, identified through a postal sift, together with their spouses outside that age group. It is designed to be representative of the population of such people living in private households in Great Britain. Full details are given in Bone *et al.* (1992).

The purpose of the survey was to identify the factors affecting the age at retirement, to gather information on the financial provisions that people make for retirement, and to predict the distribution of future pensioners' incomes. Not surprisingly, the survey found that the group receiving the highest income before retirement also received the highest income after retirement, and this group consisted mainly of people who were male, were working in non-manual occupations, did not have disabilities, and were in employment at the time of retirement. Women who had never married received pensions that were not much lower than men's; but the prolonged periods of economic inactivity associated with child-rearing and marriage meant that overall the pension income of women was much lower than that of men (the mean net retirement income of men was £108 per week, compared with £50 for women).

BASIC CHARACTERISTICS FROM RETIREMENT SURVEY

Weights are applied to the sample to take into account aspects of the sample procedure and non-response which might otherwise bias the results (see Bone *et al.*, 1992). The size of the weighted sample is close to the actual sample size and in most cases the weights are close to 1. Table A1 shows the magnitude of adjustment from the original figures to the weighted sample.

Table A1: Comparison of original sample and weighted numbers, Retirement Survey, 1988

age group	Men		Women		Both	
	original	weighted	original	weighted	original	weighted
55–59	571	575	585	586	1,156	1,161
60–64	559	547	640	612	1,199	1,159
65–69	510	507	611	608	1,121	1,115
Total	1,640	1,628	1,836	1,806	3,476	3,434

Source: Retirement Survey, Great Britain, 1988

The adjustment is very small for both men and women in the age groups 55–59 and 65–69, although slightly more, especially for women, in the age group 60–64.

Tables A2 and A3 compare weighted figures from the Retirement Survey with another large-scale survey, the General Household Survey, carried out in 1988, and with the British census of 1991.

Table A2: Sex ratios; by age group, people in Great Britain aged 55–69

	Retirement Survey			General Household Survey			1991 Census		
Age group	Men	Women	Weighted N	Men	Women	N	Men	Women	N ('000)
55–59	50	50	1,161	49	51	1,312	50	50	2,839
60–64	47	53	1,159	50	50	1,364	48	52	2,824
65–69	45	55	1,115	47	53	1,291	46	54	2,737

Sources: *Retirement Survey, 1988*
General Household Survey, 1988; Foster et al., 1990:14
Census, 1991: OPCS, 1993:14

Table A3: Marital status; people in Great Britain aged 55–69

Survey	Married/ cohabiting	Single	Widowed	Divorced/ separated	N (weighted for RS)
	%	%	%	%	
Retirement Survey	74	7	13	6	3,434
General Household Survey	77	6	14	5	3,887
Census 1991	74	7	13	6	8,400,077

Sources: *Retirement Survey, 1988*
General Household Survey, 1988; derived from Foster et al., 1990:15
Askham et al., 1992:19
Census, 1991: OPCS, 1993:33

As we would expect, partly as a result of the weighting procedure used, the demographic composition of the sample in the Retirement Survey matches the census population well. Table A2 shows that even though the General Household Survey has a larger sample size than the Retirement Survey, the sex ratio of the latter is closer to that of the census population. This is especially clear in the 60–64 year age band. Table A3 demonstrates that the marital status structure of the weighted sample of the Retirement Survey is identical to that of the population as a whole. Again, the Retirement Survey sample matches the general population better than the General Household Survey sample.

However, although the Retirement Survey is nationally representative, the sub-section of carers is small.

Table A4: Weighted sample sizes of carer groups, Retirement Survey, 1988; people aged 55–69, by gender

	Males	Females	Both
Co-resident carer	92	138	230
Other current carers	165	266	431
Past carer	390	714	1,104
Non-carer	981	689	1,670
Total	1,628	1,806	3,434

Source: *Retirement Survey, Great Britain, 1988*

Table A5: Carer status of respondents, Retirement Survey, 1988; people aged 55–69, by gender

	Men		Women		Both	
	%	Weighted N	%	Weighted N	%	Weighted N
Both current and past carer	5	86	10	180	7	246
Current carer only	12	198	15	276	14	474
Past carer only	24	390	40	713	32	1,104
Never been a carer	60	981	38	689	49	1,670

Source: *Retirement Survey, Great Britain, 1988*

Table A4 shows that of the sample of 3,434, just over half, 1,765, were currently, or had ever been, a carer. As we are interested in this study in looking specifically at differences between past carers and people who have never cared, however, it is necessary to separate current from past carers. Table A5 shows that 7% of the whole sample were currently caring for someone, and had also cared for someone in the past. Although nearly one in three were past carers only, the sample sizes are quite small – 390 men and 713 women. As we begin to classify our sample of past carers according to other factors of interest, such as retirement status and age (Table A6), some sample sizes become too small to be really useful. There are, for example, only 33 male retired past carers aged 55–59.

Sample sizes are further restricted due to missing data in some cases. For example, when calculating the number of years that past carers spent caring

Table A6: Weighted sample sizes of carer groups, Retirement Survey, 1988; by age group, gender, retirement and carer status

	Men				Women			
	Retired		Other		Retired		Other	
	Past carer	Non carer	Past carer	Non carer	Past carer	Non carer	Past carer	Non carer
55–59	33	66	85	292	78	65	127	163
60–64	68	141	59	196	181	209	50	49
65–69	142	266	4	21	255	188	22	15
ALL	242	472	148	509	515	462	199	227

Source: Retirement Survey, Great Britain, 1988

for someone, six respondents did not give the year when they first started caring, and seven did not give the year that they stopped caring. Four did not give either. All of these cases have to be omitted from any analysis which examines the length of time spent caring.

In the main text, unweighted sample numbers are given in tables since they are a better guide to the reliability of the means, medians and proportions which are based on them. These means, medians, and proportions are, of course, weighted.

STATISTICAL RELIABILITY

All findings from sample surveys are subject to sampling variation and hence to some uncertainty. This needs to be borne in mind when drawing conclusions about the general population. The smaller the sample size and the larger the variation in the variable of interest, the greater is the uncertainty.

Formal measures of the extent of this uncertainty involve the calculation of *standard errors* and their use to test the *statistical significance* of, for example, the difference between two means and to construct *confidence intervals* or margins of error, around that difference. In the main text, standard errors are given for means and medians and can be calculated for proportions using the formula:

$$s = \sqrt{(p(1-p)/n)}$$

where p is the relevant proportion and n the sample number on which it is based.

The larger the standard error in relation to the estimate in question, the greater the uncertainty in question.

The formula above, and the calculations underlying the standard errors of means and medians presented in the main body of this report, assume that the sample has been drawn using simple random sampling. In practice, most sample surveys, including the Retirement Survey, have more complex sample designs which involve clustering and multi-stage stratification. This means that the quoted standard errors will tend to understate the true standard errors and so there may be more uncertainty than is implied.

Standard errors for means have been calculated using standard formulae. For medians, the formulae used are as in, for example, Pudney and Sutherland (1992).

Printed in the United Kingdom for HMSO
Dd300751 12/94 C25 G559 10170

Published by HMSO and available from:

HMSO Publications Centre
(Mail, fax and telephone orders only)
PO Box 276, London, SW8 5DT
Telephone orders 0171-873 9090
General enquiries 0171-873 0011
(queuing system in operation for both numbers)
Fax orders 0171-873 8200

HMSO Bookshops
49 High Holborn, London, WC1V 6HB
(counter service only)
0171-873 0011 Fax 0171-831 1326
68–69 Bull Street, Birmingham, B4 6AD
0121-236 9696 Fax 0121-236 9699
33 Wine Street, Bristol, BS1 2BQ
0117 9264306 Fax 0117 9294515
9–21 Princess Street, Manchester, M60 8AS
0161-834 7201 Fax 0161-833 0634
16 Arthur Street, Belfast, BT1 4GD
01232 238451 Fax 01232 235401
71 Lothian Road, Edinburgh, EH3 9AZ
0131-228 4181 Fax 0131-229 2734

HMSO's Accredited Agents
(see Yellow Pages)

and through good booksellers